NOTEWORTHY
Listening and Notetaking Skills
Third Edition

NOTEWORTHY
Listening and Notetaking Skills
Third Edition

Phyllis L. Lim   **William Smalzer**

Australia • Canada • Mexico • Singapore • Spain • United Kingdom • United States

THOMSON
HEINLE

Noteworthy: Listening and Notetaking Skills, Third Edition
Phyllis L. Lim
William Smalzer

Publisher, Adult and Academic ESL: James W. Brown
Sr. Acquisitions Editor: Sherrise Roehr
Director of ESL and ELT Product Development:
  Anita Raducanu
Development Editor: Kasia Zagorski
Director of Marketing: Amy Mabley
Technology Manager: Andrew Christensen
Production Manager: Sarah Cogliano
Manufacturing Manager: Marcia Locke
Project Coordination and Composition:
  Pre-Press Company, Inc.
Cover Art: "Rhythme 38," 1938 by Sonia Delaunay,
© L & M SERVICES B.V. Amsterdam 20040504. Photo:
Jacqueline Hyde. Musee National d'Art Moderne,
Centre Georges Pompidou, Paris, France
© CNAC/MNAM/Dist. Reunion des Musees
Nationaux/Art Resource, NY.

Photo Manager: Sheri Blaney
Photo Researcher: Billie Porter
Cover Designer: Ha Nguyen
Text Designer: Carol Rose
Printer: Malloy Lithographing, Inc.

Printed in the United States of America.

1 2 3 4 5 6 7 8 9 07 06 05 04

For more information contact
Thomson Heinle, 25 Thomson Place,
Boston, Massachusetts 02210 USA,
or you can visit our Internet site at
http://www.heinle.com.

For permission to use material from this text or
product, submit a request online at:
www.thomsonrights.com.
Any additional questions about permissions can be
submitted by email to
thomsonrights@thomson.com.

ISBN: 1-4130-0398-2

Library of Congress Control Number: 2004105950

Contents

Preface

NOTEWORTHY is a high-intermediate level ESL/EFL listening and note-taking program with three major goals:

1. to improve listening comprehension and develop academic note-taking skills through extensive practice
2. to provide international students with a deeper, clearer understanding of life and culture in the United States
3. to increase productive skills through tasks in which students use aural input for reproduction and transfer activities in speaking and writing

Learning new vocabulary is an important part of each lesson, and several important notetaking skills are presented and practiced. However, overall we have used a content approach. The final activity of each unit is a written quiz covering the content of the three lectures in the unit.

The topics of the fifteen lectures, divided into five units, are both universal and academic in nature: population, immigration, multiculturalism, globalization, education, and government, for example. The vocabulary is mostly subtechnical, found and used across disciplines and in different professions. There is a general progression from easy to more difficult within each unit and from the beginning to the end of the book. The lectures are delivered in a relaxed, natural style of speech.

An effort is made to help students see the organization of a lecture, to see both the forest and the trees. Motivation to take good notes is built in, as students need their notes for oral activities soon after the lecture and for a quiz some time later.

Acknowledgements

The authors and publisher would like to thank the following reviewers:

Michael Berman
Montgomery College

Lois Lundquist
Harper College

Patricia Brenner
University of Washington

Marie Mitchell
Arizona State University

Jennifer Kraft
Oakland Community College

To the Teacher

Teachers will find that NOTEWORTHY offers both stimulating topics for study and great versatility. Any one of its three major goals can be emphasized to fit the needs of different classes. A teacher who chooses not to devote the extra time needed for students to take notes could use the materials for listening comprehension with a focus on cultural content. Individual lessons could be used to provide background for further treatment of a topic, and suggestions for doing so are given. And, of course, the teacher who wishes to concentrate on production could use the lectures as input for the accompanying oral and written exercises.

Note: The symbol in the margin indicates that the material needed to complete the listening activity is on the accompanying Audio CD or cassette tape.

FEATURES IN THE THIRD EDITION

- A new feature added to the third edition of NOTEWORTHY is a video component. The lecture for each chapter is now available on DVD or VHS. The video is meant to be used as a complement to the traditional audio program. Students may opt to view a chapter's lecture on video in order to simulate a more authentic classroom listening and notetaking experience.
- The audioscript for NOTEWORTHY is now conveniently located in the back of the Student Book, in Appendix A.
- The Unit Quizzes and Quiz Answer Keys are now located on the Heinle Listening and Notetaking Web site. Teachers can download them from notetaking.heinle.com.
- New topics, "Globalization" and "Distance Education," as well as updated lectures from the second edition.
- Extensive work on rhetorical cues to help students detect the organization of the lectures.
- Communicative follow-ups to lectures in which students verify their notes by asking each other questions.
- Accuracy checks that require students to refer to their notes rather than answer questions from memory.
- Transfer activities that accommodate EFL as well as ESL classes.
- Collaborative activities for writing summaries and essay question answers as well as for developing critical thinking skills.
- Suggestions for pursuing the topic.
- Quiz preparation for each unit. Students review lectures and collaborate in writing short-answer and essay exam questions.

CHAPTER OUTLINE

Provided below is an explanation of the purpose of each part of a full chapter, which requires about three 50-minute periods to complete. (Teachers who opt to do **Pursuing the Topic** will need additional periods.)

Discussion: to introduce the topic, to stimulate students' curiosity, and to begin establishing a cognitive schema for the lecture through a discussion of illustrations.

Vocabulary and Key Concepts: to familiarize students with new sub-technical vocabulary and with the major concepts of the chapter.

Predictions: to get students to invest in the lesson by predicting the content of the lecture through their questions. As students share their prediction questions with the class, a schema for the content is further established.

Notetaking Preparation: to give students strategies for understanding the organization of lectures and for taking down information in an organized manner and in a meaningful, usable form.

Listening: to lead students through a series of listenings to distinguish the main subtopics from supporting details. Some guidance is given, but content is stressed over skills, and the emphasis is on repeated practice at notetaking.

Accuracy Check: to check students' comprehension and the completeness of their notes through a ten-question short-answer quiz.

Oral Activities: to provide small-group oral practice that draws on the language and information of the lecture as input to improve students' oral competence. At the same time, students check the completeness of their notes, which they use for these activities.

Review: reconstruction of different portions of the lecture.

Transfer: questions for discussion or for an oral report on a similar topic in the students' countries.

Collaboration: to provide opportunities for students to further develop language and academic skills in small groups through discussion, summary writing, and writing answers to essay questions.

Pursuing the Topic: to offer suggestions for further study of the topic through readings, videos, the Internet, and interviews.

Unit Quiz Preparation (at the end of each unit): to help students anticipate unit quiz questions by reviewing notes in order to distinguish main ideas from supporting ones. Students write quiz questions and answer them.

Unit Quiz: to evaluate students' mastery of the skills and content taught and to simulate the college or university experience of taking a test on content. Quizzes require both short answers and essays. The Unit Quizzes are available on the Heinle Listening and Notetaking Web site: notetaking.heinle.com.

SUGGESTIONS FOR TEACHING

Discussion: Question students briefly about the photographs to get them to focus on them and to introduce the topic. Then discuss the questions as a class. Write important vocabulary on the board, if time permits. The activity should require no more than a few minutes, just enough time to introduce the topic and arouse curiosity. Time: 4–5 minutes.

Vocabulary and Key Concepts: Have students quickly read through the sentences silently before they listen to the dictated sentences on the tape. This encourages students to invest in the exercise and may be done as homework. After they listen to the tape and fill in the blanks, quickly go over the spelling of each word, and discuss the meanings of words they ask about. Time: 10–12 minutes.

Predictions: Ask students to write three questions about the possible content of the lecture so that they make more of an investment in the lesson. If the example questions aren't enough to get them started writing their own questions, ask a "leading" question or two: Do you know how many people there are in the United States? (pause) How would you write the question to find out? Time: 8–10 minutes.

Notetaking Preparation: Go over the skill in Section D.1 and have students practice the skill if appropriate. Try to move quickly, because they will practice the skill again during the lecture. Some skill exercises could also be assigned as homework, and those that require pre-lecture reading should be. Section D.2, which generally deals with the organization of the lecture, can be done as homework and checked in class to save time. Time: will vary depending on the particular skill in D.1 and whether D.2 is done in class or at home.

Listening: The text calls for two listenings per lecture and additional listening outside of class for those students who fail to get at least 70 percent on the Accuracy Check. There is nothing magical in these numbers. Students stronger in listening comprehension may do well with fewer listenings from the beginning, and weaker students may need more, especially at the beginning of the course. Take into account the general level of the class when deciding how many whole-class listenings to do. Try to maintain some pressure without pushing students to the frustration level. If possible, provide an opportunity for additional listening *outside* class. Ideally, in one class period, you should get through at least the Prelistening Activities and the First Listening. Time: depends on the length of each lecture and the number of listenings done in class. (Actual lecture times vary from about 7 minutes to about 12 minutes.)

Accuracy Check: Do as quickly as is feasible. After students listen to and answer questions by referring to their notes, discuss only those answers that students disagree on. Try to raise their consciousness about why they missed an answer: Did they misunderstand the lecture? Were their notes inaccurate? Or were they unable to locate the information in their notes? Sometimes students try to write down too much and miss relevant information. Sometimes they may simply be unable to locate information that they have in their notes. Recommendations for further listening and/or rewriting notes should be made at this time. Strive to complete and discuss the Accuracy Check by the end of the second class. Time: 12–15 minutes.

Oral Activities:

Review: Be sure that every student is involved in the activity by having individual students responsible for assigned sections of the lecture. (If students get their "assignments" the previous day, they can prepare at home and save class time.) You can vary the activity by having pairs or small groups of students prepare the same section together. Sometimes you may want individual students to report on their sections to just one other student; at other times, pairs or small groups can report to the whole class. Time: 10–25 minutes, depending on the complexity and length of the lecture and on the format you choose.

Transfer: Students in multinational classes will benefit from doing reports about their own countries on topics from the lectures. Students from the same country can work together to prepare the reports and present the information as a panel or assign one individual to present it. In either case, students should prepare brief notes to speak from rather than write out the full report. Students in homogeneous classes, such as those in EFL settings, will find class discussions more interesting and less duplicative of effort and information. Time: will vary depending on the activity chosen, class size, and number of different national groups.

Collaboration: Appoint one member of the group as a leader, one as a recorder, and one as a reporter (when appropriate). Establish realistic time limits for completing the activity. Allow enough time for sharing upon completion of the task. Each group should receive peer feedback especially for summary writing and essay question answer writing. If time is short, assign fewer questions per group for the discussion and essay question answer writing. Time: depends on which skill is being practiced and the number of questions assigned.

Pursuing the Topic: If your schedule and course design allow, you may want to use our suggestions for further study of the topic. We have tried to include suggestions for further listening, reading, and speaking, but not every topic lends itself easily to all three. The suggestions are obviously not exhaustive, but they may remind you of works that you find more suitable for use with your students. Or the students themselves can treat this activity as a research project in which they look for articles, stories, and books that they read and report to the class on. Students in an EFL setting, who will have difficulty finding informants for interviews, may be able to locate one American who would be willing to be interviewed by the whole class. Time: will vary according to the material and activities chosen.

Follow-up Activities: Keep all follow-up activities as brief as possible. Besides providing feedback, they are also meant to remind students of the purpose of the just-completed task and to provide closure before moving to the next activity. Time: 2–3 minutes.

Unit Quiz Preparation: Our experience is that students retain information better and do better on quizzes when they anticipate the questions that will be asked. Use this section to help students anticipate quiz questions by having them review their notes and then write practice short-answer and essay exam questions. To save class time, students can review their notes at home by looking at the information in terms of main ideas and details that support the main ideas within each major subtopic. In class, small groups should then be ready to write short-answer questions that focus more on the details of the lecture as well as essay exam questions that focus more on the main ideas, albeit with support from details.

Students may well benefit from a reminder about correct question form: *question word/auxiliary/subject/verb*, in most cases. You may also want to walk around and give some guidance as students work, especially in the first units, to make sure that students understand their task. It is probably advisable to tell them that the quiz you eventually give will not derive directly from their questions; at the same time, if their notes are accurate and well-organized, they will have asked many of the same questions that the authors provide in the unit quizzes. Use the follow-up as a chance for students to evaluate their comprehension/retention of the lecture. Discuss their short-answer questions; use the better ones as review. Discuss their essay questions; choose one or two for written follow-up if desired. Time: 8–10 minutes per chapter.

Unit Quizzes (Available on the Heinle Listening and Notetaking Web site http://notetaking.heinle.com: The primary purposes of the quizzes are to build motivation to take good notes and to simulate a college experience. In a college class, students take notes that they later use to study from to prepare for tests. The time interval can be rather short, or it can be quite long—several weeks, for example.

We suggest giving a quiz on each unit. Assign point values to each question. Short-answer questions obviously earn fewer points than essay questions, and you may want to weight more difficult questions with additional points. On a 25-point scale, the short-answer questions could count a total of 10 points and the essay questions, if both are assigned, a total of 15 points.

We suggest that you let students know how much each question is worth and how much time they should devote to each portion of the quiz. If the class has studied all three chapters in a unit, you will have to make a decision about the number of essay questions to require on the quiz. Depending on the level of your class and the class time you can allot to the quiz, you may choose only one of the two essay questions for each chapter or let students make their own choice.

Another decision is whether you want your students to study their notes outside class or whether they can use them during the quiz. There are good arguments on both sides of the decision, and the goals of your particular class will help you decide. Initially, you may want to let students use their notes so that the point of having complete, usable notes is made. Having students study their notes but not use them during the quiz, however, more closely duplicates the college experience. Teachers in academic preparation programs will probably want to give students this experience.

The Face of the People

The Population

Classroom Jobs
Snack — Jimmy
Blocks — Grifyn
Plants — Malissa
Pets — Andrew
Books — Raven

I. PRELISTENING

A. Discussion

Discuss the following questions with your classmates:

- Do these pictures match your idea of the makeup of the U.S. population?

- Do you think the pictures reflect the racial diversity of the country accurately?

- Do you think there are more old people or young people in the population?

- Do you think more people live in the East or in the West of the country?

B. Vocabulary and Key Concepts

Read through the sentences, trying to imagine which words would fit in the blanks. Then listen to a dictation of the full sentences, and write the missing words in the blanks.

1. Most countries take a _____ every ten years or so

   in order to count the people and to know where they are living.

2. A country with a growing population is a country that is becom-

   ing more _____.

3. A person's _____ is partly determined by skin color

   and type of hair as well as other physical characteristics.

4. The majority of the U.S. population is of European _____.

5. The _____ _____ of a country's

   population gives information about where the people are living.

6. The total population of the United States is _____

   _____ _____ many different kinds

   of people.

7. In other words, the population _____ people of

   different races and ages.

8. The average age of the U.S. population, which is a

_____ large one, has been getting _____

higher recently.

9. _____ areas are more _____

populated than rural areas. That is, they have more people per

square mile.

10. The use of antibiotics has greatly _____ the

_____ _____ throughout much of

the world.

11. A country whose _____ _____

is higher than its death rate will have an _____

population.

12. On the average, women have a higher _____

_____ than men do.

Follow-up: Check the spelling of the dictated words with your teacher.
Discuss the meanings of these words and any other unfamiliar words
in the sentences.

C. Predictions

Using the photographs and the vocabulary exercise as a starting point,
write three questions that you think will be answered in the lecture.

Examples:
- Is the number of minorities increasing or decreasing?
- Why is the average age of the U.S. population increasing?

1. _____

_____

2. _____

_____

3. _____

_____

Follow-up: After you have written your questions, share them with
your teacher and your classmates.

1. Number Notation

During today's talk you will need to write down many numbers. Some of these will be expressed as whole numbers, some as percentages, some as fractions, and some as ratios. Let's do a little practice before the lecture. Here are some examples: If you hear "thirty-seven million," you should write this *whole number* as *37 mill.* If you hear "three fourths" or "three quarters," you should write this *fraction* as *3/4.* If you hear "one out of six," you should write this *ratio* as *1:6.* If you hear "thirteen point four percent," you should write this *percentage* as *13.4%.* Let's practice.

a. _____   f. _____

b. _____   g. _____

c. _____   h. _____

d. _____   i. _____

e. _____   j. _____

Follow-up: Check your answers with your teacher by saying each one as you write it on the board.

2. Rhetorical Cues

Lecturers usually use *rhetorical cues* to help their listeners follow the lecture. A rhetorical cue is a word or even a sentence that lets us know that some important information is coming or that a new subtopic or point is being introduced. Look at these rhetorical cues, and decide in which order you will probably hear them in today's lecture. Order them from first (1) to fifth (5).

____ **a.** Another way of looking at the population . . .

____ **b.** Today we're going to talk about population . . .

____ **c.** First of all, let's take a look . . .

____ **d.** Now, to finish up . . .

____ **e.** Before we finish today . . .

Follow-up: Discuss your answers as a class.

II. LISTENING

⌒ *A. First Listening*

Listen for general ideas. After a brief introduction, the lecturer lists his
three subtopics. He then goes on to discuss each one individually. As
you listen, write down the three major subtopics in the spaces labeled
ST1, ST2, and ST3. Take down details you have time for, but make
sure you take down the subtopics.

NOTES

Introduction:

ST1 _____

ST2 _____

Follow-up: Now check your major subtopics with your teacher.

B. Further Listening

While listening again, write down necessary relevant details below the main subtopic to which they belong. Remember to use proper number notation to save time.

Follow-up: Check your notes. If you missed important information or have doubts about your notes, (1) verify them by asking a classmate questions to fill the gaps in your notes or (2) listen to the lecture a third time. When verifying your notes with a classmate, do not show each other your notes; ask specific questions to get the information you need.

Examples:
- In what regions do most people in the United States live?
- What percentage of the population is black?
- Did the lecturer say there were 6 million more women than men in the U.S. population?

This is also a good time to check to see if the lecturer answered your *Predictions* questions about the lecture.

III. POSTLISTENING

A. Accuracy Check

Listen to the following questions, and write *short answers*. Use your notes. You will hear each question one time only.

1. _____

2. _____

3. _____

4. _____

5. _____

6. _____

7. _____

8. _____

9. _____

10. _____

Follow-up: Check your answers with your teacher. If your score is less than 70 percent, you may need to listen to the lecture again or rewrite your notes so that you can understand and retrieve the information in them.

B. Oral Activities

1. Review

In pairs, use your notes to reproduce sections of the lecture. Student A will present the introduction and subtopic 1, including details, to Student B. Student B will present subtopics 2 and 3 with details to Student A. Check what you hear against your notes. If you don't understand or you disagree with what you hear, wait until your partner finishes. Then bring your notes into agreement by seeking clarification, as follows:

- Excuse me. I didn't hear your percentage for Americans of Asian origin. Could you repeat it, please?

- I don't think I agree with what you said about the five most populous states. I think the five most populous states are. . . .

- I'm afraid my notes are different from yours. . . .

2. Transfer

If your class is multinational, prepare a short oral report about the population of your country, covering the points below. Work with the other students from your country.

If your classmates are all from your country, discuss the population of your country as a class. Discuss these points:

- the size of the population and where it is distributed geographically

- the most populous regions or cities

- whether the population in your country is increasing or decreasing and why

C. Collaboration: Summary

In groups of three, with one member acting as secretary, write a one-paragraph summary of the lecture on population. Use the questions below to decide which information to include. Write the answers in complete sentences in paragraph form, but limit your summary to 125 words.

- What is the present U.S. population?

- What are the percentages of the different races that make up the U.S. population?

- Which regions and states are the most populous? Is the population more rural or urban?

- Why are there more women than men? How much higher is women's life expectancy than men's?

- Is the average age of the population increasing or decreasing?

Follow-up: Exchange summaries with at least one other group. Check if the other group has summarized the lecture in a similar fashion.

D. Pursuing the Topic

The following are recommended for a closer look at the population of the United States:

Books/Periodicals/Internet

www.census.gov
> *This Web site has hundreds of tables and some interesting articles from the 2000 census. Besides more information about the categories discussed in the lecture, you can find information on the composition of families, marital status, and employment of U.S. residents.*

Any contemporary encyclopedia in English. Look up "United States," and find a section that interests you. For example, you could choose among population, rural and urban life, history, geography, and climate.

Immigration:
Past and Present

Immigrants wait for the ferry to take them from Ellis Island to New York City (ca. 1900).

Immigrants take an oath of citizenship at a swearing-in ceremony.

I. PRELISTENING

A. Discussion

Discuss the following questions with your classmates:

- Do you think there is more or less immigration to the United States now than in the past?

- Have the countries of origin of the immigrants changed over the years?

- Do you think people's reasons for immigrating to the United States are the same today as they were in the past?

- Have people from your country immigrated to the United States? If so, how many? Why?

B. Vocabulary and Key Concepts

Read through the sentences, trying to imagine which words would fit in the blanks. Then listen to a dictation of the full sentences, and write the missing words in the blanks.

1. Throughout history, people have moved, or _____,

   to new countries to live.

2. _____ _____ can take many forms:

   those that are characterized by a shortage of rain or food are called

   _____ and _____, respectively.

3. Sometimes people immigrate to a new country to escape political

   or religious _____.

4. Rather than immigrants, the early _____ from

   Great Britain considered themselves _____; they

   had left home to settle new land for the mother country.

5. The so-called Great Immigration, which can be divided into three

   _____, or time periods, began about 1830 and

   lasted till about 1930.

6. The Industrial Revolution, which began in the nineteenth cen-

   tury, caused _____ _____ as

   machines replaced workers.

7. The _____ of farmland in Europe caused many people to immigrate to the United States, where farmland was more abundant.

8. Land in the United States was plentiful and available when the country was _____ westward. In fact, the U.S. government offered free public land to _____ in 1862.

9. The _____ of the Irish potato crop in the middle of the nineteenth century caused widespread starvation.

10. The Great Depression of the 1930s and World War II contributed to the noticeable _____ in immigration after 1930.

11. The first law that _____ the number of immigrants coming from a certain part of the world was the Chinese Exclusion Act of 1882.

12. It is important to note that in 1965 strict _____ based on nationality were eliminated.

13. At the end of the 1940s, immigration began to increase again and has, in general, risen _____ since then.

14. Will the _____ continue for non-Europeans to immigrate to the United States?

15. The U.S. immigration laws of today in general require that new immigrants have the _____ necessary to succeed in the United States because industry no longer requires large numbers of _____ workers.

Follow-up: Check the spelling of the dictated words with your teacher. Discuss the meanings of these words and any other unfamiliar words in the sentences.

C. Predictions

Using the photographs and the vocabulary exercise as a starting point, write three questions that you think will be answered in the lecture.

Examples:
- Is immigration to the United States increasing or decreasing?
- How many immigrants return to their countries of origin after a short time?

1. _____

_____

2. _____

_____

3. _____

_____

Follow-up: After you have written your questions, share them with your teacher and your classmates.

D. Notetaking Preparation

1. Dates: Teens and Tens

In dates, *teens* and *tens* (1815 and 1850, for example) are sometimes confused in listening. For teens, as in 1815, both syllables of *15* (FIF TEEN) are stressed, with heavier stress on the second syllable. For tens, as in 1850, only the first syllable is stressed (FIF ty). Write down the dates and phrases you hear. For a whole decade like the nineteen forties, write *the 1940s.*

a. _____   f. _____

b. _____   g. _____

c. _____   h. _____

d. _____   i. _____

e. _____   j. _____

Follow-up: Check your answers with your teacher by saying each one as you write it on the board.

2. Language Conventions: Countries and Nationalities

The lecturer uses the names of several countries as well as the names of the people who come from those countries. Check your knowledge of these names by completing the following chart in three minutes. A knowledge of the names of these countries and their people will help you recognize them when you hear them. Ask your instructor to pronounce the names of these countries and their people before you listen to the lecture. You will probably want to abbreviate some of these names as you take notes.

Country	People
_____	French
Germany	_____
_____	Scotch-Irish
_____	Britons; the British
_____	Danes
_____	Norwegians
	Swedes
Greece	_____
_____	Italians
_____	Spaniards
_____	Portuguese
China	_____
_____	Filipinos
_____	Mexicans
India	_____
_____	Russians
_____	Poles

Follow-up: After you check your answers with your teacher, answer these questions: Which of the above are Scandinavian countries? Which are Southern European countries? Which are Eastern European countries? Check your answers with your teacher.

II. LISTENING

A. First Listening

After a rather long introduction in which the lecturer discusses what immigration is, some general reasons that people immigrate, and the kinds of people who came to what is now the United States while it was still a colony of Great Britain, he goes on to discuss three main subtopics. In the first listening, make sure you get down the main subtopics; take down relevant details that you have time for, including those in the introduction.

NOTES

Introduction:

ST1 _____

ST2 _____

ST3 _____

Follow-up: Now check your major subtopics with your teacher.

⌓ B. Further Listening

While listening again, write down necessary relevant details below the main subtopic to which they belong. Remember to use proper number notation to save time.

Follow-up: Check your notes. If you missed important information or have doubts about your notes, (1) verify them by asking a classmate questions to fill the gaps in your notes or (2) listen to the lecture a third time. When verifying your notes with a classmate, do not show each other your notes; ask specific questions to get the information you need.

Examples: • Could you please tell me what the lecturer said about the composition of the U.S. population in the Colonial Period?
• What was said about Ireland and the crop failure?

This is also a good time to check to see if the lecturer answered your _Predictions_ questions about the lecture.

III. POSTLISTENING

🎧 A. Accuracy Check

Listen to the following questions, and write *short answers*. Use your notes. You will hear each question one time only.

1. _____

2. _____

3. _____

4. _____

5. _____

6. _____

7. _____

8. _____

9. _____

10. _____

Follow-up: Check your answers with your teacher. If your score is less than 70 percent, you may need to listen to the lecture again or rewrite your notes so that you can understand and retrieve the information in them.

B. Oral Activities

1. Review

In groups of four, practice giving sections of the lecture to each other. Take turns practicing different sections until everyone has had a chance to speak. Student A will give the introduction, Student B will give subtopic 1, and so on. Check what you hear against your notes. If you don't understand or you disagree with what you hear, wait until the speaker finishes. Then bring your notes into agreement by clarifying points of disagreement, as follows:

• Could you repeat what you said about the population during the Colonial Period?

• My notes are different from yours. You said the famine was in England, but I think you're wrong. Let's see what the others have in their notes.

2. Transfer

Discuss with your teacher and classmates reasons why people either leave your country or come to your country. Do people leave your country for economic reasons? For educational reasons? Do they usually return home? Do people come to your country to work or to study? If so, who are these people? Do any of these people become citizens? How long do they stay in your country? What are some of the benefits of having immigrants in a country? What are some of the disadvantages?

C. Collaboration: Writing Answers to Essay Questions

On the quiz at the end of this unit, there will be short-answer questions and essay questions. You will answer the short-answer questions with a few words or a sentence or two. You will answer the essay questions with a complete paragraph.

In groups of three or four, plan and write essay answers to the following questions on immigration. Appoint one member to write; all members will participate in planning and helping with the answer.

Use these guidelines:

1. Take the question and turn it into a general topic sentence to start your paragraph. For Question #1 below, you might begin: *Between 1830 and 1930, Europeans immigrated to the United States for a number of reasons.*

2. Choose specific relevant points from the lecture to support the topic sentence.

3. Make a brief outline of your answer so that when you write it you can concentrate on writing rather than remembering.

4. Write full sentences to develop your answer. (On a quiz, do not simply *list* points of support unless you run out of time.)

5. Write only the information that the question asks for. (If you do not know or are unsure of the answer to a quiz question, write a quick, brief answer to get some points, and concentrate on the other questions.)

Questions:

1. Discuss the reasons why Europeans immigrated to the United States between 1830 and 1930.

2. Describe the population of the United States during the Colonial Period.

Follow-up: Share your answers with at least one other group. Or share your answers orally as a class, and discuss the strengths in each answer.

D. Pursuing the Topic

The following are recommended for a closer look at immigration in the United States:

Books/Periodicals/Internet

Sowell, Thomas. *Ethnic America: A History.* New York: Basic Books, 1981.
> *Sowell discusses the contributions of different ethnic and racial groups in the United States.*

http://uscis.gov
> *The U.S. Citizenship and Immigration Services Web site contains statistics on immigration, interesting articles, and information on processing immigrant visas, naturalization, and so forth.*

Wernick, Allan. U.S. *Immigration and Citizenship,* revised 3rd edition. New York: Crown Publishing Group, 2002.
> *A guide for those interested in immigrating to the United States.*

Films/Videos

Avalon, Barry Levinson, director; 126 minutes, PG.
> *The film spans fifty years in the lives of a Russian immigrant family.*

Malcolm X, Spike Lee, director; 201 minutes, PG-13.
> *Biographical film of a famous African American civil rights leader; the film shows the influences, including painful white influences, on the leader's life.*

Interview

Interview someone whose parents or grandparents immigrated to the United States. Beforehand, prepare interview questions as a class to ask

- where the person immigrated from
- when and why the person immigrated
- other questions your class is interested in

Write down the answers to the questions, and share the information with your classmates.

Variation: Invite an American to visit your class, and have the whole class interview him or her by using the questions you wrote.

Americans at Work

I. PRELISTENING

A. Discussion

Discuss the following questions with your classmates:

- What is the name of the famous CEO (chief executive officer) in one of the photos?

- In which photo are the workers offering a service?

- Do you think U.S. workers are more, equally, or less productive than workers in other industrialized countries?

- How many weeks a year of vacation do you think the average U.S. worker has?

B. Vocabulary and Key Concepts

Read through the sentences, trying to imagine which words would fit in the blanks. Then listen to a dictation of the full sentences, and write the missing words in the blanks.

1. As we look at the changes over the last century, we'll use a lot of

   _____ to describe these changes.

2. While the number of people in these _____

   _____ industries went down, the number of people

   in the _____ industries went up.

3. Over the years, child labor laws became much _____

   and by 1999, it was _____ for anyone under sixteen

   to work full-time in any of the fifty states.

4. In 1900 the average _____ _____

   income was $4,200.

5. One of the important _____ most workers received

   later in the century was _____

   _____.

6. Whereas _____ and salaries rose over the century,

   the average _____ dropped.

7. People often tend to _____ the past and talk about

   "the good old days."

8. According to a 2003 _____ released by the United Nations International Labor Organization, U.S. workers are the most _____ in the world.

9. Longer working hours in the United States is a _____ trend, whereas the trend in other industrialized countries is the _____.

10. Workers in some European countries actually _____ American workers per hour of work.

11. This higher rate of productivity might be because European workers are less _____ than U.S. workers.

12. Between 1949 and 1974, increases in productivity were _____ by increases in wages.

13. After 1974, productivity increased in manufacturing and services, but real wages _____.

14. According to a recent book, the money goes for salaries to _____, to the stock market, and to corporate _____.

15. Some people say that labor _____ have lost power since the beginning of the 1980s, and that the government has passed laws that _____ the rich and weaken the rights of the workers.

Follow-up: Check the spelling of the dictated words with your teacher. Discuss the meaning of these words and any other unfamiliar words in the sentences.

C. Predictions

Using the photographs and the vocabulary exercise as a starting point, write three questions that you think will be answered in the lecture.

Examples: • How much money did U.S. workers make at the beginning of the last century?

1. _____
   _____

2. _____
   _____

3. _____
   _____

Follow-up: After you have written your questions, share them with your teacher and your classmates.

D. Notetaking Preparation

1. Abbreviations

To save time and get down more information when you listen to a lecture, it is helpful to abbreviate words. It is important to abbreviate them in a way that will allow you to remember what the full form is, of course. Another person's abbreviation may not help you remember. Practice abbreviating the following terms you will hear in the lecture in a way that you will know what each abbreviation stands for a few days or a few weeks later. Look at the examples to see how some terms from the lecture have been abbreviated.

Examples: historical look at work: hist lk at wk
statistics: stats

Term	Abbreviation
a. agriculture	_____
b. mining, manufacturing, and construction	_____
c. service industries	_____
d. wages and salaries	_____
e. average per capita income	_____
f. health insurance	_____
g. working conditions	_____
h. increased productivity	_____
i. stock market	_____
j. labor unions	_____

Follow-up: With a partner, take turns covering up the left column. Looking at the right column, practice saying the terms that your abbreviations stand for. Your partner will check your accuracy.

2. Rhetorical Cues

Lecturers usually use rhetorical cues to help their listeners follow the lecture. A rhetorical cue is a word or even a sentence that lets us know that some important information is coming or that a new subtopic or point is being introduced. Look at these rhetorical cues, and decide in which order you will probably hear them in today's lecture. Order them from first (1) to fourth (4).

_____ **a.** Then we'll look at how U.S. workers are doing today.

_____ **b.** First, we'll take an historical look at work in America.

_____ **c.** First, let's consider how the type of work people were involved in changed over the last century.

_____ **d.** Now let's turn our attention to the current situation for U.S. workers.

Follow-up: Discuss your answers as a class.

II. LISTENING

A. First Listening

Listen for general ideas. In a brief introduction the lecturer makes a few remarks about how Americans look at work, and then goes on to mention his two main subtopics.

NOTES

Introduction:

ST1 _____

Follow-up: Now check your major subtopics with your teacher.

B. Further Listening

While listening again, write down necessary relevant details below the main subtopics to which they belong. Remember to use proper number notation and abbreviations to save time.

Follow-up: Check your notes. If you missed important information or have doubts about your notes, (1) verify them by asking a classmate questions to fill the gaps in your notes or (2) listen to the lecture a third time. When verifying your notes with a classmate, do not show each other your notes; ask specific questions to get the information you need.

Examples: • How many children were in the workforce in 1900?
• What is the name of the book the lecturer mentioned?

This is also a good time to check to see if the lecturer answered your *Predictions* questions about the lecture.

III. POSTLISTENING

A. Accuracy Check

Listen to the following questions, and write *short answers*. You will hear each question one time only.

1. _____

2. _____

3. _____

4. _____

5. _____

6. _____

7. _____

8. _____

9. _____

10. _____

Follow-up: Check your answers with your teacher. If your score is less than 70 percent, you may need to listen to the lecture again or rewrite your notes so that you can understand and use them later.

B. Oral Activities

1. Review

In pairs, use your notes to reproduce sections of the lecture. Student A will present the introduction and subtopic 1 including details to Student B. Student B will present subtopic 2 including details. Check what you hear against your notes. If you don't understand or you disagree with what you hear, wait until your partner finishes. Then bring your notes into agreement by seeking clarification, as follows:

- I don't think the lecturer said 60 percent of the workforce were women in 1999.

- Could you repeat what you said about the average per capita income in 1999?

- Did you understand the meaning of "a rising trend"?

2. Transfer

If you and your classmates come from different countries, prepare a short oral report about work in your country, covering the points below. Work with other students from your country.

If your classmates are all from the same country, discuss work in your country as a class, covering the points below.

- how work changed over the last century

- what kind of work most people in your country do

- what percentage of women are employed

- how many hours a week most people work

- whether things are getting better for workers or not

C. Collaboration: Discussion

Discuss the following questions in small groups. Appoint one person to report your group's opinions to the class.

1. Do you think most people are happy to leave farms to go work in industry? Explain your answer.

2. Is there ever a good reason for children to work? Why or why not?

3. Should women have the same opportunities to be employed as men, both before and after they are married? Give reasons.

4. Should the government set the number of weeks of vacation workers get each year? Why or why not?

5. Should workers share in the profits of the companies they work for? Explain your answer.

D. Pursuing the Topic

The following are recommended for a closer look at work in the United States:

Books/Periodicals/Internet

Schor, Juliet B. *The Overworked American*. New York: Basic Books, 1993.
> *In her best-selling book, Schor concluded that Americans worked an average of one month more per year in 1990 than in 1970.*

Ciulla, Joanne B. *The Working Life*. New York: Times Books, 2000.
> *Ciulla concludes that Americans let their work define them, which is dangerous as companies generally see workers as replaceable cogs.*

Fraser, Jill Andresky. *The White-Collar Sweatshop*. New York: W. W. Norton & Company, 2002.
> *From her five years of interviews across the country with white-collar workers, Frazier describes what she believes has gone wrong and suggests possible solutions for workers.*

Films/Videos

American Dream, Barbara Kopple, director; 100 minutes, no rating.
> *The film shows the attempts of workers at a huge meat-packing plant to negotiate salaries with the help of their union.*

Interview

Interview an American who has worked at a job for at least five years. Beforehand, prepare interview questions as a class to ask. Here are some suggestions:

- where the person works
- how long he or she has worked there
- how he or she feels about the job
- what the person's favorite and least favorite parts of the job are
- four to five additional questions the class is interested in

During the interview, write down the answers to the questions, and later share the information with your classmates.

Variation: Invite an American to visit your class, and have the whole class interview him or her by using the questions you wrote.

Now that you have completed the chapters in this unit, your teacher may want you to take a quiz. Your teacher will tell you whether or not you can use your notes to answer the questions on the quiz. If you can use your notes, review them before taking the quiz so that you can anticipate the questions and know where to find the answers. If you cannot use your notes, *study them carefully before you take the quiz*, concentrating on organizing the information into main ideas and details that support these main ideas.

Work in small groups to help each other anticipate the questions your teacher will ask. Before breaking up into groups, review your notes and highlight important, noteworthy points. After reviewing your notes, break up into groups. Discuss and write specific short-answer questions and more general essay questions. Follow these guidelines in writing the questions:

Writing Short-Answer Questions

Short-answer questions . . .

- should be specific, easy to answer in a few words or two sentences at most.

- should be clearly stated so that it is obvious what answer is wanted.

- should ask for facts, not opinions or information outside the lecture.

Exercise 1

Judge these questions by the above criteria. Mark each question + if it is good and − if it is bad. Discuss reasons for your choices, citing the criteria above.

____ 1. Talk about the U.S. worker.

____ 2. Do workers in your country work harder than workers in the United States?

____ 3. What is the basic difference between the service industries and other industries?

____ 4. In 1999 what percentage of U.S. women were working?

____ 5. Compare the U.S. worker in 1900 with the U.S. worker in 1999.

Essay questions . . .

- are usually in the form of a statement.

- are more general and require at least a paragraph—that is, several sentences—to answer fully.

- usually begin with a headword such as *discuss, describe, explain, compare and contrast, list, analyze,* or *summarize.* These headwords explain the writer's purpose in answering the question:

  1. to give all sides of the topic (discuss)

  2. to give all the important details of something (describe)

  3. to make something clear by giving reasons or by explaining how to do it (explain)

  4. to write the similarities and differences (compare and contrast)

  5. to name the parts of something, one by one (list)

  6. to break something into its logical parts in order to explain it (analyze)

  7. to write something in a shorter form, giving the main ideas and omitting the details (summarize)

Exercise 2

Judge these questions by the above characteristics. Mark each question + if it is good and − if it is bad. Discuss reasons for your choices, citing the characteristics above.

____ **1.** Compare the U.S. worker in 1900 and 1999.

____ **2.** List the percentage of U.S. women who were working in 1999.

____ **3.** Discuss the child labor laws that were in place by 1999.

____ **4.** Discuss the U.S. workers today in terms of productivity and wages.

Write your group's questions on the following pages.

UNIT QUIZ PREPARATION

Unit One | **The Face of the People**

Chapter 1   **The Population**

Assign one group member to write down the questions; all members will help plan and compose the questions. For the lecture on population, write five short-answer questions that can be answered with a few words or a maximum of two sentences.

1. _____

_____

2. _____

_____

3. _____

_____

4. _____

_____

5. _____

_____

Follow-up: Write your questions on the board to discuss as a class.

Written follow-up: Prepare for the quiz by writing answers to the questions your class has proposed. You have abbreviations in your notes, but do not use abbreviations other than standard ones like *U.S.* in your answers.

UNIT QUIZ PREPARATION

Chapter 2   Immigration: Past and Present

Assign one group member to write down the questions; all members will help plan and compose the questions. For the lecture on immigration, write five short-answer questions that can be answered with a few words or sentences. In addition, write two essay questions; word the questions so that they can easily be turned into topic sentences.

Short-Answer Questions

1. _____
   _____

2. _____
   _____

3. _____
   _____

4. _____
   _____

5. _____
   _____

Essay Questions

1. _____
   _____

2. _____
   _____

Follow-up: Write your questions on the board to discuss as a class.

Written follow-up: Prepare for the quiz by writing answers to the questions your class has proposed. You have abbreviations in your notes, but do not use abbreviations other than standard ones like *U.S.* in your answers.

UNIT QUIZ PREPARATION

Chapter 3   Americans at Work

Assign one group member to write down the questions; all members will help plan and compose the questions. For the lecture on work, write five short-answer questions that can be answered with a few words or sentences. In addition, write two essay questions; word the questions so that they can easily be turned into topic sentences.

Short-Answer Questions

1. _____

   _____

2. _____

   _____

3. _____

   _____

4. _____

   _____

5. _____

   _____

Essay Questions

1. _____

   _____

2. _____

   _____

Follow-up: Write your questions on the board to discuss as a class.

Written follow-up: Prepare for the quiz by writing answers to the questions your class has proposed. You have abbreviations in your notes, but do not use abbreviations other than standard ones like *U.S.* in your answers.

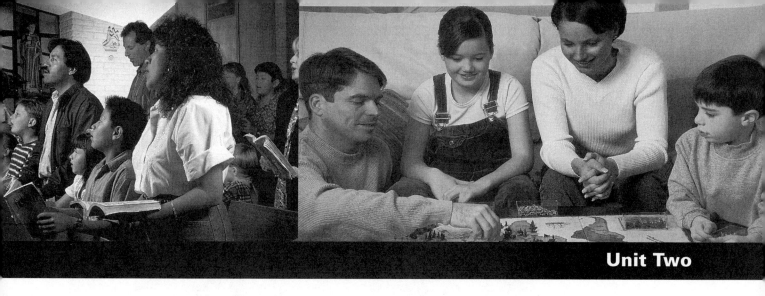

The American Character

Family in the United States

I. PRELISTENING

A. Discussion

Discuss the following questions with your classmates:

- How typical do you think the first picture is of U.S. families?
- Are single-parent families common in your country?
- Is it common for parents in your country to leave children in day care while they work?
- Who takes care of the children when parents are not home?

⌒ B. Vocabulary and Key Concepts

Read through the sentences, trying to imagine which words would fit in the blanks. Then listen to a dictation of the full sentences, and write the missing words in the blanks.

1. A hundred years ago, one heard the same comments about the family that one hears today—in short, that the American family is _____.

2. Proof of this disintegration included evidence that women were not completely content with their _____ _____.

3. To the contrary, the very _____ of the family has changed _____ in the last fifty years.

4. To be sure, the family is a very _____ _____ for what is happening in the society.

5. Demographically, the _____ _____ of the family was the traditional one.

6. The country idealized the family in these years: there was a _____ to the family and a _____ for it.

7. Three characteristics stand out in this period: _____ to social norms, greater male domination of the family, and clearcut _____ roles.

8. These decades were characterized by a

   _____ of conformity to social norms and

   included the sexual revolution and the women's

   _____ movement.

9. Another important movement was the drive for self-expression

   and _____ - _____ .

10. The new configuration of the family had to include families of

    _____ _____ , with or

    without children.

11. The number of single-parent households _____ ,

    and the number of unmarried couples _____ .

12. They see a continuing _____ in divorce

    rates since the 1980s but also a decline in birth rates after an

    _____ increase in the 1980s.

13. There is an attempt to _____ work with

    family obligations, and concern seems to be shifting from

    _____ to the new familism.

14. Places of work may offer more _____ work-

    ing hours and _____ - _____

    day care.

15. For its part, the government could _____

    parental leave and family _____ .

Follow-up: Check the spelling of the dictated words with your teacher.
Discuss the meanings of these words and any other unfamiliar words
in the sentences.

C. Predictions

Using the photograph and the vocabulary exercise as a starting point, write three questions that you think will be answered in the lecture.

Examples:
- How big are American families compared to those in other parts of the world?
- Does a divorced mother sometimes move back with her parents?

1. _____

_____

2. _____

_____

3. _____

_____

Follow-up: After you have written your questions, share them with your teacher and your classmates.

D. Notetaking Preparation

1. Key Words: Content Words

A good notetaker knows that it is neither efficient nor necessary to take down a lecture word for word. A good notetaker listens for relevant information and then uses key words to take down only the essential information. A good way to pick key words is to concentrate on the *content words* you hear: nouns, verbs, adjectives, and adverbs. (Auxiliaries, the verb *to be*, pronouns, and prepositions are *structure words*, words that receive less stress when spoken. They are less important in your notes, too.)

Practice reducing information to key words by using the sentences from Vocabulary and Key Concepts. Do sentences 5, 7, 8, 11, and 12. Sentence 2 has been done for you.

2. <u>Proof of disintegration: women not content with domestic role.</u>

_____

5. _____

_____

7. _____

_____

8. _____

_____

11. _____

_____

12. _____

_____

Follow-up: With a partner, test your key words by trying to recall all the information in the sentences from what you wrote. Your partner will check to see if you can recall the *message*, not necessarily the exact words of the original sentences. Then change roles and test your partner's key words in the same way.

2. Rhetorical Cues

Lecturers usually use *rhetorical cues* to help their listeners follow the lecture. A rhetorical cue is a word or even a sentence that lets us know that some important information is coming or that a new subtopic or point is being introduced. Look at these rhetorical cues, and decide in which order you will probably hear them in today's lecture. Order them from first (1) to fifth (5).

____ **a.** Well, let's proceed in chronological order and start with the traditional familism.

____ **b.** The third period, the new familism, is harder to see because we are living in this period now.

____ **c.** The second period, the period of individualism, saw three important social and political movements.

____ **d.** To make this point clearer, we'll take a look at how the American family has changed in the last fifty years by looking at three different time periods.

____ **e.** Because individualism is so often mentioned in our discussion of U.S. culture and people, I should make a little detour before we discuss it.

Follow-up: Discuss your answers as a class.

II. LISTENING

A. First Listening

Listen for general ideas. The lecturer looks at changes in the family over the last fifty years and divides the changes into three different periods, each with its own label. For each period, the lecturer looks at cultural, economic, and demographic aspects of the family. As you listen, decide what the three different periods are, and write them under ST1, ST2, and ST3. Take down details you have time for, but make sure you take down the subtopics.

NOTES

Introduction:

ST1 _____

ST2 _____

ST3 _____

Follow-up: Now check your major subtopics with your teacher.

B. Further Listening

While listening again, write down necessary relevant details below the main subtopic to which they belong. Remember to use key words to save time.

Follow-up: Check your notes. If you missed important information or have doubts about your notes, (1) verify them by asking a classmate questions to fill the gaps in your notes or (2) listen to the lecture a third time. When verifying your notes with a classmate, do not show each other your notes; ask specific questions to get the information you need.

Examples:
- Do you have any idea what _domestic_ means?
- Did you understand the explanation of individualism?
- How many different movements were discussed for the second period?

This is also a good time to check to see if the lecturer answered your *Predictions* questions about the lecture.

III. POSTLISTENING

A. Accuracy Check

Listen to the following questions, and write *short answers*. Use your notes. You will hear each question one time only.

1. _____

2. _____

3. _____

4. _____

5. _____

6. _____

7. _____

8. _____

9. _____

10. _____

Follow-up: Check your answers with your teacher. If your score is less than 70 percent, you may need to listen to the lecture again or rewrite your notes so that you can understand and retrieve the information in them.

B. Oral Activities

1. Review

In groups of three, use your notes to reproduce sections of the lecture. Each member of your group should bring up a point from the introduction that he or she finds interesting. Then Student A will present the information in subtopic 1, Student B the information in subtopic 2, and Student C the information in subtopic 3. If you don't understand or you disagree with what you hear, wait until your classmate finishes. Then bring your notes into agreement by seeking clarification, as follows:

- Would you mind repeating what you said about the sexual revolution? I didn't catch it.

- I don't think my notes agree with yours on the matter of cultural developments during the second period. In my notes, I wrote that. . . .

2. Transfer

If your class is multinational, prepare a short oral report about the family in your country, covering the points below. Work with the other students from your country.

If your classmates are all from your country, discuss the family in your country as a class. Discuss these points:

- Is there a predominant family configuration in your country?

- Has it changed in the last fifty years?

- What effects have economic, demographic, and cultural changes had on the family in your country?

C. Collaboration: Summary

Work with a partner, and use your notes to write a summary of the lecture in 125 words or less. Answer this question for your first main idea sentence: *Has the U.S. family changed a little or a lot in the last fifty years?* Then characterize each of the three periods by choosing relevant information about demographic, cultural, and economic points.

Follow-up: Share your summary with at least one other pair. Find something you like in each summary that you read. Alternatively, your teacher may ask for volunteers to read their summaries to the class.

D. Pursuing the Topic

The following are recommended for a closer look at the American family:

Books/Periodicals/Internet

http://unstats.un.org/
> *The United Nations Statistics Division: This site has demographic and social statistical information from around the world. From the home page, locate Demographic and Social statistics; then locate the link to World's Women 2000 to find information about women, families, wages, marriages, and other issues gathered in 2000.*

www.wellesley.edu/WomenSt/Family_Gender_Resources/web.html
> *Families and Gender Studies Resources Page: This site contains links to many other sites that deal with abortion, adoption, gay families, motherhood, reproductive technologies, work, and family social policy, among others. To find additional information and resources, do a general Internet search for the keyword* Family Studies.

Chollar, Susan. "Happy Families: Who Says They All Have to Be Alike?" *American Health*, July–August 1993, pp. 52–57.
  Chollar discusses a variety of successful family configurations.

Etzioni, Amitai. "Children of the Universe." *UTNE Reader*, May/June 1993, pp. 52–61.
  Etzioni discusses the roles of U.S. parents and government in raising children.

Kimmel, Michael. "What Do Men Want?" *Harvard Business Review*, December 1993, pp. 50–63.
  Changing economics force American men to redefine themselves, but U.S. companies aren't keeping up to allow men to take on their new roles.

Films/Videos

Mrs. Doubtfire, Chris Columbus, director; 119 minutes, PG-13.
  This comedy shows the extremes to which a father will go to be near his children after their mother divorces him.

Kramer vs. Kramer, Robert Benton, director; 105 minutes.
  A serious film that shows the break-up of a marriage and investigates the issue of child custody in such cases.

Religion

I. PRELISTENING

A. Discussion

Discuss the following questions with your classmates:

- Where do you think the people in the picture are?

- What are the people doing?

- What do you think the expression "freedom of religion" means?

- Are there many different religions in your country?

B. Vocabulary and Key Concepts

Read through the sentences, trying to imagine which words would fit in the blanks. Then listen to a dictation of the full sentences, and write the missing words in the blanks.

1. The U.S. government cannot ask for information on religious affiliation on a _____ basis.

2. One _____ done in 2002 shows that 76 percent of the total population identified themselves as Christian, with 52 percent identifying themselves as _____ and 24 percent as Catholic.

3. The number of Americans belonging to churches or other religious organizations is surprisingly high compared to other _____ nations.

4. This is not to suggest that religious _____ are not important in these other nations.

5. Freedom of worship is _____ by the First Amendment to the Constitution.

6. The First Amendment also _____ the separation of church and state.

7. The importance of religion in American history should not be _____.

8. I'd like to talk about the increasing _____ religion has _____ in fairly recent history.

9. Religion had seemed to be in _____, but there was a religious _____ in the 1970s that surprised many people.

10. The religious revival was _____ in nature and, at first, largely confined to issues in the private sphere of life.

11. These issues, however, were very _____ in nature and became quite _____ in a short time.

12. Perhaps the "rise of the religious right" is a temporary _____ in American life.

13. Some people predict that American society will become increasingly _____ and less religious in the future; others predict a more _____ political atmosphere based on conservative religious belief.

Follow-up: Check the spelling of the dictated words with your teacher. Discuss the meanings of these words and any other unfamiliar words in the sentences.

C. Predictions

Using the photograph and the vocabulary exercise as a starting point, write three questions that you think will be answered in the lecture.

Examples: • What were the controversial issues that were involved in the religious revival in the 1970s?

1. _____
   _____

2. _____
   _____

3. _____
   _____

Follow-up: After you have written your questions, share them with your teacher and your classmates.

D. Notetaking Preparation

1. Commonly Used Symbols and Abbreviations

To save time while taking notes, it is useful to use symbols and abbreviations. You may want to develop some of your own for words and phrases that you often hear. However, there are many that are commonly used that you may find very helpful. The following are some of these commonly used symbols and abbreviations. Put a check next to the ones that are new to you and that you think might be helpful in your notetaking. Refer back to this page from time to time to see if you are using all the symbols and short abbreviations that would be useful in your notetaking.

Symbols	
+	and, plus
&	and
–	less, minus
=	equals, is the same as, consists of
≠	does not equal, is different from
>	is greater than, is more than
<	is less than
–>	causes, results in, leads to
⫫>	does not cause, does not result in, does not lead to
<–	is caused by, results from
<⫫	is not caused by, does not result from
∴	therefore
∵	because, because of
↗	rises, increases
↘	goes down, decreases
'	minute, feet (e.g., 3' = 3 feet)
"	inches *or* ditto marks (repeat the word immediately above)
°	degrees
%	percent, percentage
$	dollar, money

Abbreviations (first six from Latin)	
e.g.	for example
i.e.	that is
etc.	et cetera
cf.	compare
c.	about/approximately
ca.	about/approximately
w/	with
w/o	without

Listen to and take notes on the following sentences, which contain information taken from several lectures for which you could use some of the symbols and abbreviations above. Try to take down *content words,* abbreviate as many of these content words as possible, and use your notetaking symbols and abbreviations. You will hear each item two times.

(1–3 from lecture on population)

1. _____

2. _____

3. _____

(4–5 from lecture on immigration)

4. _____

5. _____

(6–7 from lecture on American family)

6. _____

7. _____

Follow-up: (1) Compare your notes with your classmates'. Reconstruct the full message of what you heard from your notes. (2) When you finish taking notes on today's lecture on religion, look at your notes and see if there were places that you missed where you could have used a symbol such as < or a short abbreviation such as w/o to save time.

2. Rhetorical Cues

Read the following sentences, which contain rhetorical cues to help you follow the organization of the lecture. Decide in which order you will probably hear them. Number them from first (1) to fifth (5).

_____ **a.** Let's consider the first way America differs from these other modernized nations.

_____ **b.** Finally, let's take a closer look at this rise in the influence of religion on American political life.

_____ **c.** Let's take a look at two ways that religion in the United States differs from religion in other modernized nations.

_____ **d.** However, there is another somewhat contradictory difference that we should also consider.

_____ **e.** However, whether this group will be able to influence political life for a long time cannot be known.

Follow-up: Discuss your answers as a class.

II. LISTENING

A. First Listening

In the introduction the lecturer discusses the reasons for the great number of churches in the United States. At the end of the introduction he mentions the three subtopics he will go on to develop. Take down details you have time for, but be sure to take down the subtopics.

NOTES

Introduction:

ST1 _____

ST2 _____

ST3 _____

Conclusion:

Follow-up: Check your major subtopics with your teacher before you listen to the lecture for the second time.

∩ B. Further Listening

While listening again, write down necessary relevant details below the main subtopic to which they belong. Remember to use symbols and abbreviations to save time.

Follow-up: Check your notes. If you missed important information or have doubts about your notes, (1) verify them by asking a classmate questions to fill the gaps in your notes or (2) listen to the lecture a third time. When verifying your notes with a classmate, do not show each other your notes; ask specific questions to get the information you need.

Examples:
- Do you remember which is the second-largest religious group in America?
- What did the lecturer say about the First Amendment?
- What does "religious right" mean?
- Which people were surprised by the religious revival?

This is also a good time to check to see if the lecturer answered your *Predictions* questions about the lecture.

III. POSTLISTENING

∩ A. Accuracy Check

Listen to the following questions, and write *short answers*. You will hear each question one time only.

1. _____

2. _____

3. _____

4. _____

5. _____

6. _____

7. _____

8. _____

9. _____

10. _____

Follow-up: Check your answers with your teacher. If your score is less than 70 percent, you may need to listen to the lecture again or rewrite your notes so that you can understand and retrieve the information in them.

B. Oral Activities

1. Review

In pairs, use your notes to reproduce sections of the lecture. Student A will present the introduction and subtopic 1, including details, to Student B. Then Student B will present subtopics 2 and 3 with details to Student A. Check what you hear against your notes. If you don't understand or you disagree with what you hear, wait until your partner finishes. Then bring your notes into agreement by seeking clarification, as follows:

- Excuse me, what did you say about the television and film media?

- I don't think your numbers are correct.

- Could you repeat what you said about the future role of religion in America?

2. Transfer

Discuss these questions with a partner or in small groups if you and your classmates come from different countries. If not, discuss them with your teacher and classmates.

- What are the major religious groups in your country?

- What is the relationship between the government and religion in your country?

- Do you think religion is becoming more or less important in your country? Explain.

C. Collaboration: Writing Answers to Essay Questions

To help you prepare for the essay questions in the Unit Quiz at the end of this unit, in groups of three or four, plan and write essay answers to the following questions on religion in the United States. Appoint one member of the group to do the actual writing; all members of the group should participate in planning and helping with the answers. At this point, you should refer to the guidelines in Unit 1, Chapter 2, p. 18. Review the guidelines before you begin to write essay answers.

Questions:

1. Contrast religion in the United States with religion in modernized European countries.

2. Describe the conflict between the government and the religious right on the issues of legalized abortion and prayer in schools.

Follow-up: Share your answers with at least one other group. Or share your answers orally as a class, and discuss the strengths in each answer.

D. Pursuing the Topic

The following are recommended for a closer look at religion in the United States:

Books/Periodicals/Internet

Find any contemporary encyclopedia in English. Look up the names of various religious minorities in the United States, such as "Mormons," "Seventh-Day Adventists," or "Amish." Read to learn about their historical background, their major beliefs, and any problems they have had as a religious minority.

Films/Videos

Witness, Peter Weir, director; 112 minutes, R.
> *This film depicts the life of the Amish in the United States: their commitment to nonviolence and the resulting culture clash when one of them accidentally witnesses a brutal murder.*

Interview

Interview an American about his or her views on religion in America. Beforehand, prepare interview questions as a class to ask on

- religious background
- role of religion in his or her life
- his or her opinion about freedom of religion, the separation of church and state, prayer in public schools, and the relationship between politics and religion
- any other questions your class is interested in

Write down your answers to the questions, and share the information with your classmates.

Variation: Invite an American to visit your class, and have the whole class interview him or her, using the questions you wrote.

Passages:
Birth, Marriage, and Death

I. PRELISTENING

A. Discussion

Discuss the following questions with your classmates:

- Does this wedding look similar to weddings in your country?
- How do you think this couple will celebrate the birth of their baby?
- What is happening in the bottom photo?

🎧 B. Vocabulary and Key Concepts

Read through the sentences, trying to imagine which words would fit in the blanks. Then listen to a dictation of the full sentences, and write the missing words in the blanks.

1. Customs and traditions are often _____ to foreigners, partly because the customs are so _____ that most local people accept them without ever thinking about them.

2. The baby _____ is given by a close friend or relative of the _____ mother.

3. The _____-_____-_____ is often invited to someone's home on some _____ so that she can be surprised.

4. Through advice and _____ _____ _____, the expectant mother is _____ about the desirability of her situation.

5. A few years ago, it was almost _____ _____ for men to participate in baby showers.

6. In the past, men were _____ from the _____ room, but today many men are with their wives to "coach" them through the birth.

7. Christians usually have a religious service, called a

   _____, for the new baby.

8. Some customs are generally _____ concern-

   ing _____, the engagement period, and the

   wedding ceremony.

9. Because priests, rabbis, and ministers are all legally

   _____ to marry couples, it is not necessary

   to have both a _____ and a religious

   ceremony.

10. Some customs about the _____ and

    _____ are rather _____

    in nature.

11. Some churches and other places where weddings are held have

    recently _____ the throwing of rice as being

    _____ to guests, who can slip and fall on it.

12. At the time of death, one decision is whether the funeral will be

    held in a church or in a funeral home; another decision is whether

    the body will be _____ or buried in a

    cemetery.

13. The family may choose to have a _____

    service instead of a funeral. In either case, the family may hold

    a _____, where the body of the deceased

    is displayed in its casket.

14. At a funeral, a _____ is usually given by

    someone close to the _____ person.

15. Those who want to express their _____

    usually send a sympathy card to the _____

    family.

Follow-up: Check the spelling of the dictated words with your teacher. Discuss the meanings of these words and any other unfamiliar words in the sentences.

C. Predictions

Using the photograph and the vocabulary exercise as a starting point, write three questions that you think will be answered in the lecture.

Examples:
- Must a child's baptism take place in the same church that the parents were married in?
- Why are dead bodies displayed in a casket before the funeral?

1. _____

_____

2. _____

_____

3. _____

_____

Follow-up: After you have written your questions, share them with your teacher and your classmates.

D. Notetaking Preparation

1. Key Words: Listening

We have already talked about using key words to save time and take good notes. Think of key words as a *telegram*, that is, the basic information in reduced form. Practice reducing the following sentences you will hear to key words. You will hear each sentence twice. Listen, decide on the key words, and write them in the space below. For example, as you listen to the first sentence, see how the author has used key words to reduce the information.

a. ethnic groups follow old customs, but *still* general culture in U.S.

b. _____

c. _____

d. _____

e. _____

Note: The notetaker here not only reduced the number of words in the sentence greatly but also reworded it somewhat. Can *you* recreate the message of the sentence from these notes? Or would your notes look different?

Follow-up: Use your key words to reproduce the messages you heard. Add any words necessary to make your sentences clear and grammatical. Work with a partner, or check your answers as a class.

2. Adverbs as Content Words

Because adverbs are content words, it is important to understand them and to get them down in your notes. Read these sentences from the lecture, focusing on the italicized adverbs. Discuss the difference in meaning, if any, when you substitute the adverb in parentheses.

1. *Almost always* a baby shower is arranged in secret so as to be a complete surprise to the mother-to-be. (Occasionally)

2. *Usually* she was invited to someone's home on one pretext or another. (Ordinarily)

3. There is *always* a very emotional outpouring of good wishes. (often)

4. In the past, when births mainly took place at home, it was a *strictly* female event. (mainly)

5. Men *never* went into the delivery room. (rarely)

6. For Christians, this service is *ordinarily* called a baptism. (sometimes)

7. It is very hard to generalize, but there are some customs that are *quite generally* observed. (traditionally)

II. LISTENING

A. First Listening

The lecturer begins his talk with a discussion of cultural traditions in general and of how the United States is somewhat different from many countries. He then announces his subtopics: birth, marriage, and death. Because you already know the subtopics, you will have time to write down some main and secondary ideas of support in the first listening. Use key words and structure your notes.

NOTES

Introduction:

ST1 _____

ST2 _____

ST3 _____

🎧 B. Further Listening

While listening again, write down necessary relevant details below the main subtopic to which they belong. Remember to use content words as key words to save time.

Follow-up: Check your notes. If you missed important information or have doubts about your notes, (1) verify them by asking a classmate questions to fill the gaps in your notes or (2) listen to the lecture a third time. When verifying your notes with a classmate, do not show each other your notes; ask specific questions to get the information you need.

Examples:
- Can you explain what a baby shower is?
- What was said about marriage superstitions?
- What's the difference between a funeral and a memorial service?

This is also a good time to check to see if the lecturer answered your *Predictions* questions about the lecture.

III. POSTLISTENING

🎧 A. Accuracy Check

Listen to the following questions, and write *short answers*. Use your notes. You will hear each question one time only.

1. _____

2. _____

3. _____

4. _____

5. _____

6. _____

7. _____

8. _____

9. _____

10. _____

Follow-up: Check your answers with your teacher. If your score is less than 70 percent, you may need to listen to the lecture again or rewrite your notes so that you can understand and retrieve the information in them.

B. Oral Activities

1. Review

In pairs, use your notes to reproduce sections of the lecture. Student A will present the introduction and subtopic 1, including details, to Student B. Student B will present subtopics 2 and 3 with details to Student A. Check what you hear against your notes. If you don't understand or you disagree with what you hear, wait until your partner finishes. Then bring your notes into agreement by seeking clarification, as follows:

- My notes are a little different from yours. I don't believe men are allowed to come to baby showers.

- Excuse me. I didn't catch what you said about the tradition of what brides wear or carry at their weddings.

2. Transfer

Choose *one* of the major subtopics (birth, marriage, or death) and carefully describe your customs that differ from those in the United States. Your teacher may ask you to present your report orally to a small group or the whole class, or to write a paragraph to hand in.

C. Collaboration: Discussion

Discuss the questions below in small groups. Appoint one person to report your group's opinions to the class.

1. Is it surprising that people in the United States, with its great racial and ethnic diversity, celebrate birth, marriage, and death in similar ways? Why or why not?

2. Death is a topic that is very difficult for most Americans to talk about. What reasons might there be for their avoidance of the topic of death?

3. The lecturer mentioned two fairly recent changes in American society. One is that men are now sometimes invited to baby showers and the other is that more and more men accompany their wives in the delivery room when the baby is born. Do you think these are positive changes? Why or why not?

4. The lecturer discussed superstitions connected to weddings, specifically that a groom should not see the bride in her wedding dress before the ceremony. What reason might there be for this superstition? Does your culture have superstitions connected to weddings? Superstitions about births and deaths? What are they?

D. Pursuing the Topic

The following are recommended for a closer look at life passages in the United States.

Books/Periodicals/Internet

Kübler-Ross, Elisabeth. *On Death and Dying*. New York: Macmillan, 1969.
> *The author discusses terminal illness, dying, and how those involved can deal with these issues.*

Films/Videos

Father of the Bride, Charles Shyer, director; 114 minutes, PG.
> *The comedy depicts a father's reaction to his daughter's falling in love, getting engaged, and finally getting married.*

Steel Magnolias, Herbert Ross, director; 118 minutes, PG.
> *A sentimental look at marriage, motherhood, and the lives of women in a small Louisiana town.*

UNIT QUIZ DIRECTIONS

Now that you have completed the chapters in this unit, your teacher may want you to take a quiz. Your teacher will tell you whether or not you can use your notes to answer the questions on the quiz. If you can use your notes, review them before taking the quiz so that you can anticipate the questions and know where to find the answers. If you cannot use your notes, *study them carefully before you take the quiz,* concentrating on organizing the information into main ideas and details that support these main ideas.

Work in small groups to help each other anticipate the questions your teacher will ask. Before breaking up into groups, review your notes and highlight important, noteworthy points. After reviewing your notes, break up into groups. Discuss and write specific short-answer questions and more general essay questions. (For guidelines in writing questions, see the Unit Quiz Directions at the end of Unit 1.)

Write your group's questions on the following pages.

UNIT QUIZ PREPARATION

Unit Two | **The American Character**

Chapter 4   Family in the United States

Assign one group member to write down the questions; all members will help plan and compose the questions. For the lecture on the family, write five short-answer questions that can be answered with a few words or sentences. In addition, write two essay questions; word the essay questions so that they can easily be turned into topic sentences.

Short-Answer Questions

1. _____
   _____

2. _____
   _____

3. _____
   _____

4. _____
   _____

5. _____
   _____

Essay Questions

1. _____
   _____

2. _____
   _____

Follow-up: Write your questions on the board to discuss as a class.

Written follow-up: Prepare for the quiz by writing answers to the questions your class has proposed. You have abbreviations in your notes, but do not use abbreviations other than standard ones like *U.S.* in your answers.

UNIT QUIZ PREPARATION

Chapter 5   Religion

Assign one group member to write down the questions; all members will help plan and compose the questions. For the lecture on religion, write five short-answer questions that can be answered with a few words or a maximum of two sentences. In addition, write two essay questions; word the essay questions so that they can easily be turned into topic sentences.

Short-Answer Questions

1. _____
   _____

2. _____
   _____

3. _____
   _____

4. _____
   _____

5. _____
   _____

Essay Questions

1. _____
   _____

2. _____
   _____

Follow-up: Write your questions on the board to discuss as a class.

Written follow-up: Prepare for the quiz by writing answers to the questions your class has proposed. You may have abbreviations in your notes, but do not use abbreviations other than standard ones like *U.S.* in your answers.

UNIT QUIZ PREPARATION

Chapter 6   Passages: Birth, Marriage, and Death

Assign one group member to write down the questions; all members will help plan and compose the questions. For the lecture on passages, write five short-answer questions that can be answered with a few words or sentences. In addition, write two essay questions; word the questions so that they can easily be turned into topic sentences.

Short-Answer Questions

1. _____

   _____

2. _____

   _____

3. _____

   _____

4. _____

   _____

5. _____

   _____

Essay Questions

1. _____

   _____

2. _____

   _____

Follow-up: Write your questions on the board to discuss as a class.

Written follow-up: Prepare for the quiz by writing answers to the questions your class has proposed. You may have abbreviations in your notes, but do not use abbreviations other than standard ones like *U.S.* in your answers.

American Trademarks

Multiculturalism

A patchwork quilt

A crucible

I. PRELISTENING

A. Discussion

Discuss these questions with your classmates:

- Why do you think the crucible and the patchwork quilt are often used as symbols of the multicultural character of U.S. society?

- What does the crucible do to different metals mixed in it?

- Is the culture of your country heterogeneous, as in the United States, or homogeneous?

B. Vocabulary and Key Concepts

Read through the sentences, trying to imagine which words would fit in the blanks. Then listen to a dictation of the full sentences, and write the missing words in the blanks.

1. I understand why a foreigner might react _____

    to U.S. culture, especially if the person comes from a more

    ethnically and racially _____ society.

2. It seems naive or even perverse to _____

    the existence of a culture that has such great _____

    on other cultures, for better or worse.

3. A _____ pot, literally a pot in which metals

    like aluminum and copper are melted in order to blend them, is

    the traditional _____ for the way the differ-

    ent groups of immigrants came together in the United States.

4. Some people feel that the monoculturalist view of many national-

    ities blending together into an _____ of all

    the parts in it is a _____.

5. Opponents point out that many groups have at times been

    _____ from participating in U.S. society

    through segregation and _____.

6. U.S. society probably did not assimilate new cultural input until

    the new immigrants were _____ with less

    _____.

7. The metaphor the multiculturalists use is the patchwork quilt, a

    _____ of separate, _____

    subcultures.

8. _____ and the _____

    of children of another race make a difference in how people in a

    family look at themselves.

9. The point here is that the ethnically and racially pure individuals

    _____ by the multiculturalist view are

    more the _____ than the rule.

10. We _____ some of our culture from our

    families and _____ some of our culture

    unconsciously.

11. If _____ does not take place in the first

    _____, it most certainly does by the second

    or third.

12. Monoculturalists fear a _____, or even

    destruction, of U.S. culture, whereas _____

    of the pluralistic view disagree.

13. It would be wrong to assume that the _____

    culture we've been speaking about _____

    the culture of only one group.

14. _____ of the pluralistic view of culture cite

    _____, especially Mexican immigrants, the

    single largest immigrant group since the 1990s.

Follow-up: Check the spelling of the dictated words with your teacher.
Discuss the meanings of these words and any other unfamiliar words
in the sentences.

C. Predictions

Using the photographs and the vocabulary exercise as a starting point, write three questions that you think will be answered in the lecture.

Examples: • Is U.S. culture becoming more like the cultures of new immigrants?
• Is American culture basically European?

1. _____

_____

2. _____

_____

3. _____

_____

Follow-up: After you have written your questions, share them with your teacher and your classmates.

D. Notetaking Preparation

1. Key Words: Listening

Work with a partner to practice taking down key words: nouns, verbs, adjectives, and adverbs. One partner will read *Vocabulary and Key Concepts* sentences 1–4 while the other takes notes. Then switch parts for sentences 5–8.

Follow-up: With your partner, test your key words by recalling all the information in the sentences from what you wrote. Your partner will check to see if you can recall the *message*, not necessarily the exact words. Then change roles and test your partner's key words.

2. Rhetorical Cues: Transition Words

Formal speech, like formal writing, is characterized by more frequent use of transition words and phrases. Transition words like *however*, *therefore*, and *in fact* help the listener understand the relationship between the lecturer's ideas. A good understanding of transition words will make a formal lecture more coherent to you. Test your knowledge of the italicized words on the next page by using them to complete the sentences in the exercise.

- *Nevertheless, on the other hand,* and *however* all point out contrasts between two ideas.

- *For instance* presents examples.

- *In fact* is used for emphasis.

- *Rather* is used like *instead.*

- *Furthermore* is used like *also.*

    a. The United States is not a racially homogeneous society;

    _____, Japan is.

    b. The melting pot metaphor is a very old one. _____,

    it's been used for well over a century.

    c. Culture comes to people in different ways.

    _____, we inherit some, we absorb

    some, and we choose some.

    d. There are many proponents of the multiculturalist view;

    _____, I don't really agree with this view.

    e. The multiculturalists don't use the metaphor of the melting

    pot. _____, they use the patchwork quilt.

    f. Monoculturalists fear a fragmentation of U.S. culture because of

    a massive Latino immigration. _____,

    pluralists see the bright side of this immigration.

    g. There are two problems with this theory. Some existing groups

    were excluded from participating fully in society;

    _____, newly arrived groups were

    discriminated against.

Follow-up: Discuss your answers as a class.

Culture note: "Latino" is now a more a frequent way to refer to a Spanish- or Portuguese-speaking resident in the U.S. The use of "Hispanic" to refer to someone who speaks Spanish is objectionable to many Spanish-speaking people who feel no particular connection to Spain and to those who have no connection at all to Spain. ("Hispanic" was used in Chapter 1 to be consistent with the terminology in the 2000 census.)

II. LISTENING

⌒ A. First Listening

Listen for general ideas. The lecturer begins with some objections to current views of U.S. culture, views that she finds naive. The main part of the lecture is a discussion of three different views of multiculturalism, and these views might sound similar at first. However, they are quite different, if only in subtle ways. Listen for these three different views, and write them down under ST1, ST2, and ST3. Take down details you have time for, but make sure you take down the subtopics.

NOTES

Introduction:

ST1 _____

ST2 _____

ST3 _____

Follow-up: Now check your major subtopics with your teacher.

B. Further Listening

While listening again, write down necessary relevant details below the main subtopic to which they belong. Remember to use key words to save time.

Follow-up: Check your notes. If you missed important information or have doubts about your notes, (1) verify them by asking a classmate questions to fill the gaps in your notes or (2) listen to the lecture a third time. When verifying your notes with a classmate, do not show each other your notes; ask specific questions to get the information you need.

Examples: • By any chance, did you catch what was said about the impact of U.S. culture on the world?
• Could you help me out? What does "in all fairness" mean?

This is also a good time to check to see if the lecturer answered your *Predictions* questions about the lecture.

III. POSTLISTENING

A. Accuracy Check

Listen to the following questions, and write *short answers.* Use your notes. You will hear each question one time only.

1. _____
2. _____
3. _____
4. _____
5. _____
6. _____
7. _____
8. _____
9. _____
10. _____

Follow-up: Check your answers with your teacher. If your score is less than 70 percent, you may need to listen to the lecture again or rewrite your notes so that you can understand and retrieve the information in them.

B. Oral Activities

1. Review

In groups of four, use your notes to reproduce sections of the lecture. Student A will present the introduction, Student B subtopic 1, and so on. Check what you hear against your notes. If you don't understand or you disagree with what you hear, wait until your classmate finishes. Then bring your notes into agreement by seeking clarification, as follows:

- I beg your pardon, but I didn't catch what you said about the impact of the United States on other countries.

- I'm sorry. I don't believe I followed what you said about discrimination against certain groups.

2. Transfer

If your class is multinational, prepare a short oral report about the culture of your country, covering the points below. Work with the other students from your country.

If your classmates are all from your country, discuss the culture of your country as a class. Discuss these points:

- Is your culture racially and ethnically homogeneous or heterogeneous?

- How open is your culture to influences from other cultures? Do people who spend long periods of time in your country assimilate to the culture, or do they maintain their own cultures?

- What metaphor do you think fits your culture?

C. Collaboration: Summary

In groups of three, with one member acting as secretary, write a one-paragraph summary of the lecture on multiculturalism. Use the guidelines below to decide which information to include. Write the answers in complete sentences in paragraph form, but limit your summary to 100 words.

1. Write a first general sentence that tells how many views of culture the lecturer mentions and tell whether the views are similar or different.

2. Characterize each view briefly. Mention the metaphor used to describe it as well as its main characteristics.

Follow-up: Exchange summaries with at least one other group. Find something you like in other groups' summaries. Alternatively, each group can read its summary to the class, which can then vote on the best one.

D. Pursuing the Topic

The following are recommended for a closer look at the multicultural nature of the United States:

Books/Periodicals/Internet

Postrel, Virginia I. "Uncommon Culture." *Reason*, May 1993, pp. 67–69.
    Postrel discusses how and why assimilation takes place in the United States.

Rodriguez, Richard. *Days of Obligation: An Argument with My Mexican Father.* New York: Viking, 1992.
    Rodriguez, born of Mexican immigrant parents, discusses his controversial views of U.S. multiculturalism.

Search under the terms *multiculturalism* or *pluralism* for thousands of Web sites, many of which originate from or relate to many countries around the world besides the United States, including Australia, Canada, Nepal, India, and the United Arab Emirates, among many others.

Films/Videos

The Joy Luck Club, Wayne Wang, director; 138 minutes, R.
> *The movie charts the lives and loves of four Chinese immigrants and their American-born daughters.*

Mississippi Masala, Mira Nair, director; 118 minutes, R.
> *The movie explores the lives of Asian Indians living in the rural U.S. South and their dealings with African American and white communities around them.*

Crime and Violence in the United States

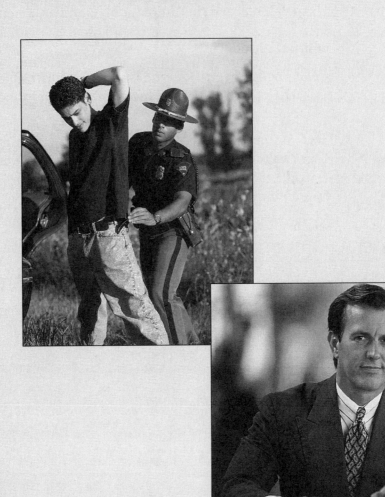

I. PRELISTENING

A. Discussion

Discuss these questions with your classmates:

- What's happening in the first picture?

- Does the man in the second picture look like a criminal? What is a white-collar crime?

- Would you say there is more crime in the United States or in your country? Why?

🎧 B. Vocabulary and Key Concepts

Read through the sentences, trying to imagine which words would fit in the blanks. Then listen to a dictation of the full sentences, and write the missing words in the blanks.

1. Between 1994 and 2001, _____ crime—

   homicide, rape, arson, and aggravated _____—

   fell 52 percent.

2. At the same time, in recent years there has been stricter law

   _____ in cities like New York and Boston,

   and very _____ penalties have been

   imposed on repeat offenders.

3. Statistics are harder to come by for _____-

   _____ crime, crimes including

   _____ and bribery.

4. One theory says that people are basically _____

   by nature and, therefore, _____

   _____ violence.

5. If a person commits a crime, society is _____

   _____ because society's _____

   are the cause of the criminal behavior.

6. There are _____ causes like racism and

   more obvious causes like the breakdown of the family and a

   _____ of drugs.

7. Because they have been _____

_____ the benefits that most Americans

have, criminals are alienated from society, which causes them

to _____ _____ at

the society.

8. The _____ is that small part of the popula-

tion that typically fits the following profile: poor, unemployed,

badly educated, _____ black, inner-city

youth, some of whom belong to gangs.

9. According to the theory, society _____ this

aggressiveness and potential violence by _____

us.

10. Society gives us _____ against killing and

stealing, for example, and values for honesty and

_____ .

11. If we are adequately socialized, we have a

_____ , the result of values that determine

how we _____ _____

our children.

12. The amount of crime depends on how _____

is used as a _____ to crime—that is, how

effectively the criminal justice system functions.

13. Typically, white-collar criminals, who include some businessmen

and _____ , may be _____

a well-developed conscience.

14. Without a strong conscience, a person's innate aggressiveness

_____ _____ and

_____ _____ crime.

15. Many experts feel that this can come about only if the underclass

has the same _____ that the majority of the

population _____ _____

_____ .

Follow-up: Check the spelling of the dictated words with your teacher. Discuss the meanings of those words and any other unfamiliar words in the sentences.

C. Predictions

Using the photographs and the vocabulary exercise as a starting point, write three questions that you think will be answered in the lecture.

Example: • How did the underclass in the United States develop?

1. _____

_____

2. _____

_____

3. _____

_____

Follow-up: After you have written your questions, share them with your teacher and your classmates.

D. Notetaking Preparation

1. Structuring

It is easier to *get* information from your notes if you make an effort to organize the ideas on the page as you *take* notes. Organizing the ideas means putting the ideas down in a logical way. The first step in organizing your ideas is to distinguish between main ideas and secondary ideas. Organize your notes by writing main ideas all the way to the left of the page and by writing secondary ideas a little to the right. Details can be indented even further to the right. Look at how the introduction to this lesson has been structured, and answer the questions that follow.

Crime statistics match public's perception of less crime

- 1994–2001: violent crime decreased 52%
  - 1994: 51 victims per 1,000
  - 2001: 24   "   "   "
- Possible reasons for decrease
  - Stricter law enforcement in cities
  - Stringent penalties on repeat offenders
- Statistics on white-collar crime (embezzlement, bribery, and so on) not as clear
  - Statistics hard to get.
  - It doesn't scare people.

  a. What is the main idea of the introduction?

  b. How many ideas (secondary) support the main idea? What are they?

  c. How many details support the secondary ideas? What are they?

Follow-up: Now check your answers with your teacher.

2. Rhetorical Cues

Read these sentences, in which the lecturer uses rhetorical cues to make a transition from one topic to another. Decide in which order you will hear them. Number them from first (1) to sixth (6).

_____ **a.** To start off with, liberals—in politics, sociology, and other fields—typically embrace the first theory.

_____ **b.** Actually, I feel that both theories serve us in identifying solutions.

_____ **c.** Crime is such a difficult issue to discuss because it can be looked at in so many different ways. Today I'd like to take a philosophical, sociological look at society and crime by discussing two theories of crime.

_____ **d.** In another lecture, we'll look at the justice system.

_____ **e.** So we need to look a little further into the causes of crime; let's look at the second theory.

_____ **f.** The second theory, often embraced by conservatives, sees people as innately aggressive and predisposed to violence.

Follow-up: Discuss your answers as a class.

II. LISTENING

🎧 A. First Listening

You already have notes for the introduction. Review those notes so that you can follow how the notetaker structured the information. Then use the first listening to take down the three major subtopics. As you take down additional information, structure it by putting main ideas to the left and indenting for secondary ideas and indenting even further for details.

NOTES

Introduction:

ST1 _____

Follow-up: Now check your major subtopics with your teacher.

B. Further Listening

While listening again, write down necessary relevant details below the main subtopic to which they belong. Remember to structure the information as you take it down.

Follow-up: Check your notes. If you missed important information or have doubts about your notes, (1) verify them by asking a classmate questions to fill the gaps in your notes or (2) listen to the lecture a third time. When verifying your notes with a classmate, do not show each other your notes; ask specific questions to get the information you need.

Examples:
- Do you have any idea whether liberals embrace the first theory or the second one?
- I'm wondering if you caught *how* society socializes people.

This is also a good time to check to see if the lecturer answered your *Predictions* questions about the lecture.

III. POSTLISTENING

A. Accuracy Check

Listen to the following questions, and write *short answers*. Use your notes. You will hear each question one time only.

1. _____

2. _____

3. _____

4. _____

5. _____

6. _____

7. _____

8. _____

9. _____

10. _____

Follow-up: Check your answers with your teacher. If your score is less than 70 percent, you may need to listen to the lecture again or rewrite your notes so that you can understand and retrieve the information in them.

B. Oral Activities

1. Review

In groups of four, use your notes to practice giving one section of the lecture to classmates. Take turns practicing different sections until everyone has had a chance to speak. For example, Student A will give the introduction, Student B will give subtopic 1, and so on. Check what you hear against your notes. If you don't understand or you disagree with what you hear, wait until the speaker finishes. Then bring your notes into agreement by clarifying points of disagreement, as follows:

- Would you mind repeating what you said about why crime is a difficult issue to discuss?

- Excuse me. Can you tell me once again why society is to blame, according to the first theory?

2. Transfer

If your class is multinational, prepare a short oral report about crime in your country, covering the points below. Work with the other students from your country.

If your classmates are all from your country, discuss crime in your country as a class. Discuss these points:

- How much crime is there in your country?

- Is the crime rate increasing or decreasing?

- What are the causes of crime?

- What solutions would you propose to reduce crime?

C. Collaboration: Writing Answers to Essay Questions

On the quiz at the end of this unit, there will be short-answer questions and essay questions. You will answer the short-answer questions with a few words or a sentence or two. You will answer the essay questions with a complete English paragraph.

With a partner, plan and write essay answers to the questions on crime. One will write the answer down, but both partners will collaborate in forming the answers.

Essay Questions

1. Contrast the two theories about the causes of crime in the United States.

2. Discuss how society socializes us, according to the second theory of crime.

Follow-up: Share your answers with at least one other group. Or share your answers orally as a class, and discuss the strengths in each answer.

D. Pursuing the Topic

The following are recommended for a closer look at crime in the United States:

Books/Periodicals/Internet

Reiss, Albert J. and Roth, Jeffrey A. *Understanding and Preventing Violence.* Washington, DC: National Academy Press, 1993.
> *The book, which you can read in the electronic version on the Internet, helps to better understand the causes of crime and provides intelligent advice about curbing it. It isn't as current as some materials but is a good investigation of the problem.*

Films/Videos

Boyz 'N the Hood, John Singleton, director; 111 minutes, R.
  The film shows young African American males who live in a world where physical and psychological violence are a constant threat.

Of Mice and Men, Gary Sinise, director; 110 minutes, PG-13.
  From a John Steinbeck novel, the film depicts the difficulties of two itinerant workers, one of whom commits a murder.

The Fugitive, Andrew Davis, director; 127 minutes, PG-13.
  A remake of an earlier movie and a TV series, this film shows a falsely accused man who escapes the police to prove himself innocent of his wife's murder.

Globalization

I. PRELISTENING

A. Discussion

Discuss these questions with your classmates:

- The first illustration on the previous page shows a "sweatshop." Why do you think the word *sweat* is part of the name? Where do we find sweatshops? How do they come about?

- What are the people in the second photo upset about?

- What are the International Monetary Fund (IMF) and the World Bank? What do they do?

- How is the World Trade Organization (WTO) different from these two banks?

B. Vocabulary and Key Concepts

Read through the sentences, trying to imagine which words would fit in the blanks. Then listen to a dictation of the full sentences, and write the missing words in the blanks.

1. The King of Bhutan said that he wasn't sure his country had one

   of those but was interested in knowing what a

   _____ _____

   _____ was.

2. Globalization is the _____ and

   _____ of economic interaction among the

   people, companies, and governments of different nations.

3. But it is at the same time a subject that _____

   the anger and mistrust of many people in the world: environ-

   mentalists, unionists, anarchists, and some governments—

   all _____ rather than supporters of

   globalization.

4. Some skeptics feel that globalization allows rich countries to take

   _____ of poor countries, which these skep-

   tics feel are only hurt by trying to be more _____.

5. And globalization is definitely about capitalism: its goal is to increase the _____ _____ _____ and capital around the world.

6. If globalization is included in a book that focuses on the United States, it is because the world sees the United States (and, to a lesser degree, Western Europe and Japan) as the _____ _____ behind the process of globalization.

7. Often, poor countries are pressured to follow global trade rules as a condition for a loan or for aid. For example, a poor country might be advised to adjust the value of its _____, or it might be advised to eliminate _____, or taxes, on goods imported from other countries.

8. _____ on new inventions and copyright laws most often protect technology from the West—and keep the technology from being used more freely by poor countries. Poorer countries may also be told to _____ their industries and banks.

9. To get an idea how these rules can in some cases _____ development instead of encouraging it, let's take a look at some countries that are not big Western powers but have _____ into the world economy—by *not* following the rules.

10. It is common for critics to claim that globalization has only _____ rich Western countries, but this claim is _____.

11. Harvard economist Dani Rodrik, in "Trading in Illusions," writes that all four countries have taken advantage of opportunities to _____ in world trade, that is, to _____ integration in the world economy.

12. India was, and still is, one of the most _____ economies in the world but has made great progress economically, and South Korea and Taiwan had patent and copyright _____ and restrictions on foreign _____—but still prospered.

13. The poor countries _____ _____ against agricultural _____ by rich countries, which make the poor countries' products less competitive in the world market.

14. The twenty-three countries did not manage to _____ the subsidies at that meeting because the talks broke down, but they did _____ _____ for themselves.

C. Predictions

Using the photographs and the vocabulary exercise as a starting point, write three questions that you think will be answered in the lecture.

Examples:
- Do most countries benefit or suffer from globalization?
- Have any poor countries prospered because of globalization?

1. _____

_____

2. _____

_____

3. _____

_____

Follow-up: After you have written your questions, share them with your teacher and your classmates.

1. Structuring

In Chapter 8, you worked on structuring your notes to make them easier to read. Practice organizing ideas again on a new topic. While listening, write the main idea on the first line under **Notes.** You will hear five examples; notice there are five equally indented lines for those, marked with diamonds (♦). The lines that are even further indented to the right are for details of two of the examples. Listen to this passage two times, and take notes using key words.

Notes

_____

♦ _____

♦ _____

♦ _____

_____

_____

♦ _____

_____

_____

♦ _____

2. Rhetorical Cues

Carefully read these sentences, which signal a transition to a new topic. Then decide in which order you will probably hear them in today's lecture. Number them first (1) to fifth (5).

_____ **a.** To get on to my second point today, let's look more closely at some non-Western countries that have achieved long-term economic growth in the past decades.

_____ **b.** To finish up by talking about our third point today, we have to take up two problems that critics of globalization bring up all the time.

_____ **c.** Let me begin this lecture by telling you a story to put things in perspective.

_____ **d.** To conclude, in my estimation, globalization is probably going to continue because capitalism has become the dominant world economic system.

_____ **e.** We can't really go into cultural imperialism today, but we can look at three different aspects of globalization to understand this complicated process a little better.

Follow-up: Discuss your answers as a class.

II. LISTENING

🎧 A. First Listening

Listen for general ideas. The lecturer has a very long introduction, giving us definitions and background that we'll need to follow the lecture. Then he explains how he will organize the lecture. The first two subtopics are quite long, whereas the third is relatively short. The conclusion is rather long because the lecturer attempts to bring all three points together. As you listen, decide what the three main subtopics are, and write them down under ST1, ST2, and ST3. Ideas in the introduction and conclusion are also important in this lecture, so try to take down important background information including the definitions.

Notes

Introduction:

ST1 _____

ST2 _____

ST3 _____

Conclusion:

Follow-up: Now check your major subtopics with your teacher.

B. Further Listening

While listening again, write down necessary relevant details below the main subtopic to which they belong. Use key words to save time, and structure the information to organize your notes.

Follow-up: Check your notes. If you missed important information or have doubts about your notes, (1) verify them by asking a classmate questions to fill the gaps in your notes or (2) listen to the lecture a third time. When verifying your notes with a classmate, do not show each other your notes; ask specific questions to get the information you need.

Examples:
- Did you get down all five examples under the first subtopic?
- What did the lecturer say about South Korea and Taiwan?
- Did the lecturer mention any countries in connection to sweatshops?

This is also a good time to check to see if the lecturer answered your _Predictions_ questions about the lecture.

III. POSTLISTENING

A. Accuracy Check

Listen to the following questions, and write *short answers* where possible. Use your notes. You will hear each question one time only.

1. _____
2. _____
3. _____
4. _____
5. _____
6. _____
7. _____
8. _____
9. _____
10. _____

Follow-up: Check your answers with your teacher. If your score is less than 70 percent, you may need to listen to the lecture again or rewrite your notes so that you can understand and retrieve the information in them.

B. Oral Activities

1. Review

In groups of five, use your notes to reproduce sections of the lecture. Student A will present the introduction, Student B, subtopic 1; student C, subtopic 2; student D, subtopic 3; and student E, the conclusion. If you don't understand or you disagree with what you hear, wait until your classmate finishes. Then bring your notes into agreement by seeking clarification, as follows:

- I didn't understand your definition of globalization. Could you repeat it?

- Is the lecturer for or against child labor? It's not clear to me.

2. Transfer

Look into your country's integration into the world economy by researching one or more of these topics:

- imports and exports, including whether subsidies and tariffs exist

- their country's economic health today compared to ten or twenty years ago and the reasons for the change if there is one

- recent participation by their country in WTO talks

- a particular World Bank or IMF project: its success and, if possible, the global trade rules imposed to complete the project

Use the library, the Internet, or an interview with an expert for information to prepare a five-minute talk to present to the class. Put the research into your own words and speak from notes (rather than read a text) to be easier to understand.

C. Collaboration: Discussion

Discuss one or two of the following questions with a partner. Then share your views with another pair or the whole class.

1. Do you think the world in general is worse off or better off because of globalization? Explain.

2. Can poorer countries oppose the will of stronger ones when it comes to world trade? If so, how?

3. Do you feel that the only ones benefiting from globalization are transnational corporations (multinationals)? Explain.

D. Pursuing the Topic

Books/Periodicals/Internet

www.guardian.co.uk/globalisation/story
   A number of different views on globalization from a British newspaper site (note the British spelling "globalisation" in the address).

   On the Internet, search under "Dani Rodik" for a Harvard professor's further views on globalization.

Films/Videos

Life and Debt, Stephanie Black, director; 86 minutes, not rated.
   A documentary which examines how the Jamaican economy has changed under the influence of the IMF, World Bank, and other organizations. Based on the book A Small Place *by Jamaica Kincaid.*

UNIT QUIZ DIRECTIONS

Now that you have completed the chapters in this unit, your teacher may want you to take a quiz. Your teacher will tell you whether or not you can use your notes to answer the questions on the quiz. If you can use your notes, review them before taking the quiz so that you can anticipate the questions and know where to find the answers. If you cannot use your notes, *study them carefully before you take the quiz*, concentrating on organizing the information into main ideas and details that support these main ideas.

Work in small groups to help each other anticipate the questions your teacher will ask. Before breaking up into groups, review your notes and highlight important, noteworthy points. After reviewing your notes, break up into groups. Discuss and write specific short-answer questions and more general essay questions. (For guidelines in writing questions, see the Unit Quiz Directions at the end of Unit 1.)

Write your group's questions on the following pages.

UNIT QUIZ PREPARATION

Unit Three | **American Trademarks**

Chapter 7   Multiculturalism

Assign one group member to write down the questions; all members will help plan and compose the questions. For the lecture on multiculturalism, write five short-answer questions that can be answered with a few words or sentences. In addition, write two essay questions; word the essay questions so that they can easily be turned into topic sentences.

Short-Answer Questions

1. _____

_____

2. _____

_____

3. _____

_____

4. _____

_____

5. _____

_____

Essay Questions

1. _____

_____

2. _____

_____

Follow-up: Write your questions on the board to discuss as a class.

Written follow-up: Prepare for the quiz by writing answers to the questions your class has proposed. You may have abbreviations in your notes, but do not use abbreviations other than standard ones like *U.S.* in your answers.

UNIT QUIZ PREPARATION

Chapter 8   Crime and Violence in the United States

Assign one group member to write down the questions; all members will help plan and compose the questions. For the lecture on crime, write five short-answer questions that can be answered with a few words or a maximum of two sentences. In addition, write two essay questions; word the essay questions so that they can easily be turned into topic sentences.

Short-Answer Questions

1. _____
   _____

2. _____
   _____

3. _____
   _____

4. _____
   _____

5. _____
   _____

Essay Questions

1. _____
   _____

2. _____
   _____

Follow-up: Write your questions on the board to discuss as a class.

Written follow-up: Prepare for the quiz by writing answers to the questions your class has proposed. You may have abbreviations in your notes, but do not use abbreviations other than standard ones like *U.S.* in your answers.

UNIT QUIZ PREPARATION

Chapter 9   Globalization

Assign one group member to write down the questions; all members will help plan and compose the questions. For the lecture on globalization, write five short-answer questions that can be answered with a few words or sentences. In addition, write two essay questions; word the questions so that they can easily be turned into topic sentences.

Short-Answer Questions

1. _____

   _____

2. _____

   _____

3. _____

   _____

4. _____

   _____

5. _____

   _____

Essay Questions

1. _____

   _____

2. _____

   _____

Follow-up: Write your questions on the board to discuss as a class.

Written follow-up: Prepare for the quiz by writing answers to the questions your class has proposed. You may have abbreviations in your notes, but do not use abbreviations other than standard ones like *U.S.* in your answers.

Education

Public Education:
Philosophy and Funding

I. PRELISTENING

A. Discussion

Discuss the following questions with your classmates:

- What kind of school do you think this is, public or private?

- Who do you think pays for the education that the children who attend this school receive?

- Where do most parents in your country prefer to send their children, to private or public schools?

⌒ B. Vocabulary and Key Concepts

Read through the sentences, trying to imagine which words would fit in the blanks. Then listen to a dictation of the full sentences, and write the missing words in the blanks.

1. Education in the United States is _____

   until a certain age or grade level.

2. A small percentage of students attend private schools, either religious or _____, but most attend public

   schools.

3. There is no nationwide _____, nor are there

   nationwide _____ examinations set by the

   federal government.

4. The federal government influences public education by providing

   _____ for special programs such as educa-

   tion for the _____ and bilingual education.

5. Control of education in the United States is mainly

   _____ _____.

6. Each state has many school districts run by school boards whose

   members are _____ by voters of the

   district.

7. The amount of funding supplied by the state and by the local

   school districts _____ over time and from

   state to state.

8. Public schools are funded to _____

   _____ _____ by local

   taxes.

9. Government funding of private schools, which are generally

   religious schools, is now and has been _____

   for some time.

10. Charter schools are _____ public schools

    that _____ with regular public schools for

    students.

11. Charter schools operate under _____ to a

    sponsor, usually a state or local school board, to whom they are

    _____ .

12. _____ of the voucher concept believe that

    private schools offer better education.

13. _____ of the voucher concept claim that

    using tax money for private schools _____

    the separation of church and state built into the U.S. Constitution.

14. The federal government in 2002, passed an educational

    _____ that requires states that wish

    to receive certain federal funding to develop and put in place

    extensive testing programs and other systems to ensure

    "_____ _____

    _____" of students.

Follow-up: Check the spelling of the dictated words with your teacher.
Discuss the meanings of these words and any other unfamiliar words
in the sentences.

C. Predictions

Using the photograph and the vocabulary exercise as a starting point, write three questions that you think will be answered in the lecture.

Example: • What are the other responsibilities of the local school districts?

1. _____

_____

2. _____

_____

3. _____

_____

Follow-up: After you have written your questions, share them with your teacher and your classmates.

D. Notetaking Preparation

1. Structuring: Outlining

A good notetaker structures his or her notes. As you develop this skill, add numbers and letters to show the organization of your notes. Part of this chapter's lecture is presented here for you to practice this skill before you listen to the complete lecture. Complete the outline below with information from subtopic 1. *Some* information is included in this outline to help keep you on track. Fill in the rest as you listen. Take a minute now to look over the outline to see where you need to fill in information.

ST1 Three levels of control

A. _____

    1. Sets basic curriculum

    2. _____

B. School district

    1. Numbers depend on _____

    2. Responsibilities
        a. _____
        b. _____
        c. _____

C. _____

    1. Teachers' responsibilities

        a. _____

        b. _____

2. Rhetorical Cues

Read the following sentences, which contain rhetorical cues to help you follow the organization of the lecture. Decide in which order you will hear them. Number them from first (1) to sixth (6).

____ **a.** Control of education in the United States is mainly exercised locally at three levels. Let's begin with the state department of education.

____ **b.** The first issue deals with the inequality of educational opportunities that students face.

____ **c.** Finally, I'd like to discuss three issues related to the funding of schools that have been receiving a lot of attention recently in the United States.

____ **d.** The second level of control is the school district.

____ **e.** The second issue is the issue of funding for private schools.

____ **f.** The third level of control is the individual school itself.

II. LISTENING

🎧 A. First Listening

Listen for general ideas. After an introduction in which the lecturer mentions distinguishing features of public education in the United States, she goes on to discuss the three levels of control on education within each state. You already have notes on ST1 in Section 1 D.1. She then goes on to explain how funding contributes to local control. Finally, she discusses three important issues related to how public education is funded. As you listen, write the subtopics in the appropriate places and details you have time for. Structure your notes like the example in Section 1. D.1.

NOTES

Introduction:

ST1 _____

ST2 _____

Follow-up: Check your major subtopics with your teacher before you listen to the lecture for the second time.

B. Further Listening

While structuring the notes, write down remaining relevant information.

Follow-up: Check your notes. If you missed important information or have doubts about your notes, (1) verify them by asking a classmate questions to fill the gaps in your notes or (2) listen to the lecture a third time. When verifying your notes with a classmate, do not show each other your notes; ask specific questions to get the information you need.

Examples:
- Who is responsible for the hiring of teachers? Is it the school district or the individual school itself?
- Where does the largest percentage of money for the public schools come from? Is it from the state or the local school district?
- What are the major differences between charter schools and voucher schools?

This is also a good time to check to see if the lecturer answered your *Predictions* questions about the lecture.

III. POSTLISTENING

A. Accuracy Check

Listen to the following questions, and write *short answers*. You will hear each question one time only.

1. _____
2. _____
3. _____
4. _____
5. _____
6. _____
7. _____
8. _____
9. _____
10. _____

Follow-up: Check your answers with your teacher. If your score is less than 70 percent, you may need to listen to the lecture again or rewrite your notes so that you can understand and use them later.

B. Oral Activities

1. Review

In groups of four, use your notes to reproduce sections of the lecture. Student A will present the introduction, and Student B will present subtopic 1, including details. Student C will present subtopic 2 with details and Student D, subtopic 3 with details. Check what you hear against your notes. If you don't understand or you disagree with what you hear, wait until the speaker finishes. Then bring your notes into agreement by seeking clarification, as follows.

- Excuse me, can you tell me what two functions of the state government are?

- Could you repeat what you said about public education in the nineteenth century?

- I'm afraid my notes about taxes are different from yours.

2. Transfer

Discuss with a classmate how the educational system in your country is different from that in the United States. Try to use some of the ideas and vocabulary from Vocabulary and Key Concepts—for example, *nationwide curriculum, standardized examinations, required courses, electives, control, compulsory.*

C. Collaboration: Summary

Work with a partner, and use your notes to write a summary of the lecture in no more than 125 words. Be sure to include information about public and private schools, funding and control of schools, and current issues in U.S. public education.

Follow-up: Share your summary with at least one other pair. Tell the other pair what you particularly like about their summary.

D. Pursuing the Topic

The following are recommended for a closer look at public education issues in the United States:

Books/Periodicals/Internet

www.ed.gov
> *Explore the Web site of the U.S. Department of Education to find out about current topics in public education.*

http://nces.ed.gov
> *Explore the Web site of the National Center for Education Statistics to find current statistics and research on education in the United States.*

Films/Videos

Stand and Deliver, Roman Menendez, director; 104 minutes, PG.
> *This film is based on the true story of a high school teacher who tried to inspire students and raise academic standards in a U.S. inner-city, minority neighborhood school.*

Dead Poets' Society, Peter Weir, director; 129 minutes, PG.
> *This film depicts the efforts of a teacher who uses poetry to inspire private preparatory school students to be more expressive and to "seize the moment," with unexpected dramatic results.*

Interview

Interview a U.S. citizen who attended public schools to find out his or her view on some of the issues highlighted in the lecture. Beforehand, write questions as a class to ask

- the person's opinion of his or her public school education

- what he or she thinks are the best and worst things about public schools

- what the person thinks about tax money in the form of vouchers going to private schools

- what he or she thinks about prayer in public schools

- any other questions your class is interested in

Write down the answers to the questions, and share the information with your classmates.

Variation: Invite an American to visit your class, and have the whole class interview him or her using the questions that you wrote.

Field Trip

If you are studying in the United States, it may be possible for your instructor to make arrangements for your class to visit a local public elementary, middle, or high school. Although the details of such visits have to be worked out with the school you visit, American students will be curious about your country and culture, so be prepared to answer questions.

Postsecondary Education:
Admissions

I. PRELISTENING

🎧 A. Discussion

Discuss the following questions with your classmates:

- Do you think that this is an important examination that the students are taking?

- What will happen if they fail this exam?

- Do students in your country take a lot of exams? What are the most important exams they take?

🎧 B. Vocabulary and Key Concepts

Read through the sentences, trying to imagine which words would fit in the blanks. Then listen to a dictation of the full sentences, and write the missing words in the blanks.

1. _____ education in the United States includes _____ as well as four-year colleges, most of which are _____.

2. To be _____, a college must meet certain _____ set by institutional and professional associations.

3. The more _____ private schools are more _____—that is, they have stiffer admissions requirements.

4. All college applicants must submit a _____ of high school grades and often _____ test results.

5. A student's _____ activities and possibly _____ _____ are often factors in his or her admission.

6. Among the 2.8 million high school graduates in 2002, 65.2 percent _____ _____ in college the following October.

7. If we _____ _____ the statistics racially, we find that white students enrolled in college in greater _____ than black or Hispanic students.

8. They may be people who attend part-time to _____ their _____, people who are changing careers, or retired people who still have a desire to learn.

9. Because most young American students have not traveled in other countries, they are not very _____ in international matters, and foreign students often find them friendly but not very _____ about their countries or cultures.

10. Some students begin college at a community college with more _____ _____ admissions requirements and later _____ _____ to a four-year college.

Follow-up: Check the spelling of the dictated words with your teacher. Discuss the meanings of these words and any other unfamiliar words in the sentences.

C. Predictions

Using the photograph and the vocabulary exercise as a starting point, write three questions that you think will be answered in the lecture.

Example: • How many colleges and universities are there in the United States?

1. _____

_____

2. _____

_____

3. _____

_____

Follow-up: After you have written your questions, share them with your teacher and your classmates.

1. Structuring: Listening

In the previous lesson we talked about *structuring* notes by using letters and numbers to make the notes clearer and easier to use. Practice structuring your notes as you listen to a portion of this lecture. Remember to move from left to right as you take down more specific information. The main idea, the most general one, is written for you.

ST3 Community colleges differ from four-year colls.

    A.

        1.

    B.

        1.

        2.

    C.

        1.

        2.

Conclusion:

Follow-up: Compare your notes with another student's. Do you have the same information under A, B, and C?

2. Acronyms

Acronyms are abbreviations in which the first letters of the words in a phrase are used as a shortcut way to speak or write about the phrase. For example, ESL is an acronym for "English as a Second Language." It is often used in both spoken and written language.

In this lecture the following tests and degrees will be referred to in abbreviated form. As you now write the first-letter abbreviations, say them to yourself. When you take notes, use the abbreviations.

Tests and Degrees	Abbreviations
Graduate Record Examination	GRE
Graduate Management Admissions Test	
Law School Admissions Test	
Medical College Admissions Test	
Scholastic Aptitude Test	
Associate of Arts degree	A.A. degree
Bachelor of Science degree	
Bachelor of Arts degree	

II. LISTENING

A. First Listening

The lecturer appears to be in a hurry today to get into her topic. Her introduction is very brief and basically consists of an announcement of her major subtopics. You will not need to take notes on the introduction itself. However, notice as you listen that the conclusion, which begins with "in brief," contains important logical conclusions about the four subtopics that you will want to include in your notes. As you take notes, take down details you have time for, but make sure that you take down the subtopics. Again, practice structuring your notes by using letters and numbers.

NOTES

ST1 _____

ST2 _____

ST3 _____

ST4 _____

Conclusion:

Follow-up: Check your major subtopics with your teacher. Which subtopic would you look under to answer the following questions?

- What are two factors that a college or university might use to decide whether to admit a student?

- What is the range (from low to high) of the total cost of attending a college or university?

- Where can you receive an Associate of Arts degree?

⌒ B. Further Listening

While continuing to structure your notes, write down remaining relevant information.

Follow-up: Check your notes. If you missed important information or have doubts about your notes, (1) verify them by asking a classmate questions to fill the gaps in your notes or (2) listen to the lecture a third time. When verifying your notes with a classmate, do not show each other your notes; ask specific questions to get the information you need.

Examples:
- What does SAT stand for? Do all high school students have to take this exam before they can graduate?
- What percentage of university students actually graduate?
- What do you have in your notes about the differences between community colleges and four-year colleges and universities? I'm not sure I got everything the lecturer said.

This is also a good time to check to see if the lecturer answered your *Predictions* questions about the lecture.

III. POSTLISTENING

⌒ A. Accuracy Check

Listen to the following questions, and write *short answers*. You will hear each question one time only.

1. _____

2. _____

3. _____

4. _____

5. _____

6. _____

7. _____

8. _____

9. _____

10. _____

Follow-up: Check your answers with your teacher. If your score is less than 70 percent, you may need to listen to the lecture again or rewrite your notes so that you can understand and use them later.

B. Oral Activities

1. Review

In small groups, review your notes section by section to be sure that all members have a complete set of notes for each subsection. At the end of this activity, your teacher will ask various class members to reproduce sections of the lecture for the whole class to listen to. At that time, check what you hear against your notes. If you don't understand or you disagree with what you hear, wait until the speaker finishes. Then bring your notes into agreement by seeking clarification, as follows:

- Did you say that some schools have up to 15,000 students or 50,000 students?

- In my notes I have that it's expensive to attend a community college. What do you have?

- I'm not sure what it means to "drop out" of school.

2. Transfer

If you and your classmates come from different countries, discuss these questions with a partner or in small groups. If not, discuss them with the whole class.

- How many colleges and universities are there in your country?

- What kinds of colleges and universities do you have?

- Where are these schools located—in major cities or in small towns?

- Approximately how many students are there at these schools?

- What percentage of high school graduates go on to a university?

Some countries take a more elitist approach to education than does the United States. That is, some countries limit the number of students who can go on to college by means of a highly competitive examination system. Discuss the following two questions in pairs, in small groups, or as a class:

- What might be some of the social, political, and economic reasons for an elitist educational system?

- What are the advantages and disadvantages of the two different approaches to education—elitist and nonelitist?

C. Collaboration: Writing Answers to Essay Questions

To help you prepare for the essay questions in the Unit Quiz at the end of this unit, plan and write essay answers to the following questions on U.S. postsecondary education in groups of three or four. Appoint one member of the group to do the actual writing; all members of the group should participate in planning and helping with the answers. At this point, you should refer to the guidelines in Unit 1, Chapter 2, p. 18. Review the guidelines before you begin to write essay answers.

Questions:

1. Discuss the wide variety of sizes, kinds, and locations of American universities and colleges.

2. Compare and contrast junior colleges and four-year universities.

Follow-up: Share your answers with at least one other group that has written on the same question(s). Or share your answers orally as a class, and discuss the strengths in each answer.

D. Pursuing the Topic

The following are recommended for a closer look at university admissions issues in the United States:

Book/Periodicals/Internet

www.collegeboard.com
This Web site gives reliable information on more than 1,500 colleges and universities to help students select a school. The site allows students to compare different colleges by listing tuition and fees, admissions requirements, and the range of students' SAT scores to let applicants know how competitive the school is. It also gives information about SAT administration, hints about applying to colleges, and information on loans and scholarships.

Distance Education

I. PRELISTENING ACTIVITIES

A. Discussion

Discuss these questions with your classmates:

- Which classroom is traditional?

- Where do you think the students are in the bottom photo?

- Would you like to be able to receive instruction at home on your TV or computer, or would you prefer to learn in a traditional classroom?

🎧 B. Vocabulary and Key Concepts

Read through the sentences, trying to imagine which words would fit in the blanks. Then listen to a dictation of the full sentences, and write the missing words in the blanks.

1. Can you imagine getting a college, or university, degree

   without ever once _____

   _____ on a college campus?

2. "Distance education is _____ that occurs

   when the instructor and student are _____

   by time or distance, or both."

3. As early as 1840, it was possible to take a _____

   course in shorthand.

4. *Peterson's 1994 Guide to Distance Learning* listed ninety-three

   _____ distance education programs

   available at _____ colleges and universities

   across the United States and Canada.

5. First, rapidly changing economic conditions require many profes-

   sional people to _____ their knowledge

   or skills on an almost _____ basis.

6. At the same time that the demand for postsecondary education

   is growing, many U.S. colleges and universities are facing

   _____ _____.

7. Millions of people have _____ to audio, video, and computer _____.

8. The _____ of instruction can _____ greatly.

9. CD-ROMs may come to the student _____ _____ or the student may _____ materials from the Internet.

10. Many distance education programs have a _____ requirement.

11. The _____ rate from distance education courses and programs is higher than for _____ courses and programs.

12. There are many _____ and disreputable universities advertising on the Internet with very _____ Web sites.

13. It is very important for anyone wishing to take a course or to pursue a degree to check out the _____ of the school they are considering very carefully.

Follow-up: Check the spelling of the dictated words with your teacher. Discuss the meaning of these words and any other unfamiliar words in the sentences.

C. Predictions

Using the photographs and the vocabulary exercise as a starting point, write three questions that you think will be answered in the lecture.

Example: • How many universities or colleges offer distance education programs?

1. _____

2. _____

3. _____

Follow-up: After you have written your questions, share them with your teacher and your classmates.

D. Notetaking Preparation

1. Deciphering Notes

Sometimes you may for one reason or another miss a lecture and have to ask a classmate to share his or her notes. If your classmate has taken good notes, you may be able to reconstruct much of the message of a lecture. Imagine that you missed a lecture in which your professor discussed some points that people interested in distance education (DE) should consider. Because you were absent, you photocopied a classmate's notes. See if you can use these notes to answer your teacher's questions. Work with a partner, if possible.

Six Things for People Int'd in DE to Consider

1. many DE programs have residency req

2. DE courses and progs have time limits

3. admissions reqs same as on-campus ed

4. DE can save money

   —Don't need to travel to class

   —But academic fees same as trad ed

   —Res reqs can be costly

5. online DE means stud needs access to comp with min reqs

   —e.g., latest version of Windows, a microph, snd card & speakers,
   adequate hard drive & RAM, modem, browser, & Internet.

   —Connection speed very imp and many schools recommend cable modem or DSL

6. stud need to be disc and ind

   —DE not easier than trad ed

   —dropout rate higher than trad ed

Directions: Answer the following questions in complete sentences.

1. Do all distance education programs have a residency requirement?

2. Is it easier to be admitted to a distance program than to on-campus programs?

3. What are three examples of computer requirements that online study might require?

4. Are students more likely to complete distance education programs or traditional programs?

2. Rhetorical Cues

Read the following sentences, which contain rhetorical cues to help you follow the organization of the lecture. Decide in which order you will hear them. Number them from first (1) to sixth (6).

____ **a.** To start with, why is distance education growing at such an incredible rate?

____ **b.** Number 1. Many distance education programs have a residency requirement.

____ **c.** Today let's look at the reasons why distance education is growing so rapidly, how distance education works, that is, what the modes of delivery are, and what some of the things people considering distance education need to be aware of.

____ **d.** Before I close today, let me just say that many people are still suspicious of distance education believing that it cannot possibly be equivalent to a traditional classroom education.

____ **e.** First, rapidly changing economic conditions require many professional people to upgrade their knowledge or skills on an almost continuous basis.

____ **f.** Students interested in pursuing distance education need to consider the following six points.

Culture note: In this lecture you will hear the following words all used interchangeably to mean <u>postsecondary education</u>: *college, university, school.*

II. LISTENING

🎧 A. First Listening

The lecturer begins with an introduction to the concept of distance education with some noteworthy historical information. He then announces his main subtopics concerning distance education (which you have already seen in the Rhetorical Cues exercise above). He then goes on to give quite a lot of detail on each subtopic. Write down as much detail as possible while structuring your notes.

NOTES

Introduction:

ST1 _____

ST2 _____

ST3 _____

Follow-up: Check your major subtopics with your teacher before you listen to the lecture for the second time.

🎧 B. Further Listening

Continue to structure your notes as you take down remaining relevant information.

Follow-up: Check your notes. If you missed important information or have doubts about your notes, (1) verify them by asking a classmate questions to fill the gaps in your notes or (2) listen to the lecture a third time. When verifying your notes with a classmate, don't show each other your notes; ask questions to get the information you need.

Examples:
- Which university offered the first correspondence catalog?
- Can you explain the difference between bulletin boards and chat rooms?
- What does disreputable mean?

This is also a good time to check to see if the lecturer answered your *Predictions* questions about the lecture.

III. POSTLISTENING ACTIVITIES

🎧 A. Accuracy Check

Listen to the following questions, and write *short answers*. You will hear each question one time only.

1. _____
2. _____
3. _____
4. _____
5. _____
6. _____
7. _____
8. _____
9. _____
10. _____

Follow-up: Check your answers with your teacher. If your score is less than 70 percent, you may need to listen to the lecture again or rewrite your notes so that you can understand and use them later.

B. Oral Activities

1. Review

In groups of four, use your notes to reproduce sections of the lecture. Student A will present the introduction. Student B will present subtopic 1, including details. Student C will present subtopic 2, and so on. Continue until all subsections, including their details, have been presented. Check what you hear against your notes. If you don't understand or you disagree with what you hear, wait until each group member has presented his or her section of the lecture. Then bring your notes into agreement by seeking clarification, as follows:

- I don't think the lecturer said that all U.S. colleges and universities have distance education courses and programs.

- Did you understand the difference between *synchronous* and *asynchronous*?

- Could you repeat what the lecturer said about admission to distance courses and programs?

2. Transfer

If you and your classmates come from different countries, discuss these questions with a partner or in small groups. If not, discuss them with the whole class.

- What kind of distance education is available in your country?

- Do you expect distance education to become more popular in your country in the future? Why or why not?

C. Collaboration: Discussion

Discuss the following questions about distance education issues in small groups. Appoint one person to report your group's opinions to the class.

1. What do you think the advantages of distance education are? What are the disadvantages?

2. Do you think distance education will ever become as common as traditional education?

3. How can students in other countries find out about distance education opportunities in such countries as the United States?

D. Pursuing the Topic

The following are recommended for a closer look at distance education in the United States:

Books/Periodicals/Internet

Bear, John B., & Bear, Mariah P. *Bears' Guide to Earning Degrees by Distance Learning.* Berkeley, CA: Ten Speed Press, 2001.

Criscito, Pat. *Barron's Guide to Distance Learning.* Hauppauge, NY: Barron's Educational Service, Inc., 2002.

Peterson's Guide to Distance Learning Programs. Lawrenceville, NJ: Petersons, a part of the Thomson Corporation, 2002.

http://www.usnews.com
> *This USNews Web site has a page dedicated to education in the United States. It allows you to browse e-learning courses, certificates, and degrees in a variety of subject areas.*

http://educationusa.state.gov
> *This U.S. government Web site is designed to provide information for international students interested in distance education.*

UNIT QUIZ DIRECTIONS

Now that you have completed the chapters in this unit, your teacher may want you to take a quiz. Your teacher will tell you whether or not you can use your notes to answer the questions on the quiz. If you can use your notes, review them before taking the quiz so that you can anticipate the questions and know where to find the answers. If you cannot use your notes, *study them carefully before you take the quiz,* concentrating on organizing the information into main ideas and details that support these main ideas.

Work in small groups to help each other anticipate the questions your teacher will ask. Before breaking up into groups, review your notes and highlight important, noteworthy points. After reviewing your notes, break up into groups. Discuss and write specific short-answer questions and more general essay questions. (For guidelines in writing questions, see the Unit Quiz Directions at the end of Unit 1.)

Write your group's questions on the following pages.

UNIT QUIZ PREPARATION

Unit Four | **Education**

Chapter 10   Public Education: Philosophy and Funding

Assign one group member to write down the questions; all members will help plan and compose the questions. For the lecture on the philosophy and funding of public education, write five short-answer questions that can be answered with a few words or sentences. In addition, write two essay questions; word the questions so that they can easily be turned into topic sentences.

Short-Answer Questions

1. _____

   _____

2. _____

   _____

3. _____

   _____

4. _____

   _____

5. _____

   _____

Essay Questions

1. _____

   _____

2. _____

   _____

Follow-up: Write your questions on the board to discuss as a class.

Written follow-up: Prepare for the quiz by writing answers to the questions your class has proposed. You may have abbreviations in your notes, but do not use abbreviations other than standard ones like *U.S.* in your answers.

UNIT QUIZ PREPARATION

Chapter 11   Postsecondary Education: Admissions

Assign one group member to write down the questions; all members will help plan and compose the questions. For the lecture on postsecondary education, write five short-answer questions that can be answered with a few words or one or two sentences. In addition, write two essay questions; word the questions so that they can easily be turned into topic sentences.

Short-Answer Questions

1. _____
   _____

2. _____
   _____

3. _____
   _____

4. _____
   _____

5. _____
   _____

Essay Questions

1. _____
   _____

2. _____
   _____

Follow-up: Write your questions on the board to discuss as a class.

Written follow-up: Prepare for the quiz by writing answers to the questions your class has proposed. You may have abbreviations in your notes, but do not use abbreviations other than standard ones like *U.S.* in your answers.

UNIT QUIZ PREPARATION

Chapter 12   Distance Education

Assign one group member to write down the questions; all members will help plan and compose the questions. For the lecture on distance education, write five short-answer questions that can be answered with a few words or one or two sentences. In addition, write two essay questions; word the questions so that they can easily be turned into topic sentences.

Short-Answer Questions

1. _____

_____

2. _____

_____

3. _____

_____

4. _____

_____

5. _____

_____

Essay Questions

1. _____

_____

2. _____

_____

Follow-up: Write your questions on the board to discuss as a class.

Written follow-up: Prepare for the quiz by writing answers to the questions your class has proposed. You may have abbreviations in your notes, but do not use abbreviations other than standard ones like *U.S.* in your answers.

The Official Side

13 The Role of Government in the Economy

I. PRELISTENING

A. Discussion

Discuss the following questions with your classmates:

- Do you think this oil field is owned by the U.S. government or by a private company?

- Are such industries (oil, gas, electricity) privately or publicly owned in your country?

- Do you think the U.S. government plays an active role in the nation's economy?

- Does your government play an active role in your country's economy?

🎧 B. Vocabulary and Key Concepts

Read through the sentences, trying to imagine which words would fit in the blanks. Then listen to a dictation of the full sentences, and write the missing words in the blanks.

1. One of the important characteristics of American-style capitalism is individual _____ of _____, including such things as houses and land, businesses, and intellectual property such as songs, poems, books, and inventions.

2. The second characteristic is _____ _____.

3. The idea in a pure capitalistic system is for the government not to _____, that is, for the government to take a _____-_____ attitude.

4. In a pure capitalistic system, the government's role would be severely limited. It would be responsible only for laws governing _____ and property, as well as for the _____ _____.

5. Companies may have to install pollution _____

   equipment to _____ _____

   government regulations.

6. People who earn little or no _____ can

   receive _____ _____,

   often called _____.

7. The government makes sure that the marketplace stays

   _____ through its _____

   and _____ laws.

8. The government interferes with the economy in an effort

   to maintain _____.

9. Through _____, the government tries

   to control _____.

10. The government has to be very careful to keep _____

    and inflation in _____, however.

11. The government further tries to achieve stability through its

    _____and by controlling the

    _____ rate.

12. Republicans, the more _____ party, tend to

    _____ fewer taxes, less welfare to the poor,

    and conditions that help business grow.

13. The government's role in the economy is not a _____

    thing because the _____ of the government

    changes every few years.

Follow-up: Check the spelling of the dictated words with your teacher. Discuss the meanings of these words and any other unfamiliar words in the sentences.

C. Predictions

Using the photograph and the vocabulary exercise as a starting point, write three questions that you think will be answered in the lecture.

Example: • How does the government make sure that businesses obey environmental protection regulations?

1. _____

_____

2. _____

_____

3. _____

_____

Follow-up: After you have written your questions, share them with your teacher and your classmates.

D. Notetaking Preparation

1. Prelecture Reading

Most U.S. college and university teachers plan their lectures assuming that students will have read assigned chapters before class. To prepare for this chapter's lecture, read the following text describing the ongoing debate about the role of the government, and answer the questions that follow. Notice that a distrust of the government has been seen in all aspects of American politics and economic life since the days of the colonies; however, this text focuses on the debate about the role of the government in the economic life of the country.

Text:

Americans have been debating the role of the federal government ever since the American Revolution in the 1770s. The thirteen original colonies, which banded together to declare their independence from Britain, were very suspicious of a strong central government and protective of their individual rights as states. The Confederation government they formed saw the thirteen original colonies through the Revolution.

A few years after the end of the war, though, the Confederation was unable to solve many problems facing the new nation, and the need for a stronger central government led to a new Constitution, which expanded the power of the national government. Still, the debate about the role of government went on in many areas, including the economic sphere. Thomas Jefferson, third President, was a believer in laissez-faire economics; that is, he believed the government should not interfere in the economy. His general philosophy was "Government that governs least, governs best."

But by today's standards, the role of the national, or federal, government in the economy was very small, consisting largely of setting tariffs and excise taxes as well as issuing currency. It wasn't until the time of the Civil War in the 1860s that the first income tax was instituted. Before that time, the government did not have money for internal improvements to the country.

After that time, the government began to expand its role in the economy. The Industrial Revolution, which was occurring at the same time, led to demands for the government to expand its role in the regulation of railroads and other big business. During these years the government tended to take the side of big business rather than the side of organized labor. During the early years of the twentieth century, the government began to debate its role in the economy more sharply. President Theodore Roosevelt and President Woodrow Wilson took steps toward controlling the excessive power of big business.

However, it was the Great Depression of the 1930s that led most people to give up the idea of a laissez-faire economy. President Franklin Roosevelt led the government to take an increased role in the welfare of the people. His "New Deal" instituted programs by which the government provided employment for large numbers of unemployed people and provided welfare for others. His administration also instituted the Social Security system, by which workers pay into a fund that then provides a kind of insurance protection for older, retired workers and disabled workers. In the years following the New Deal, the role of the government in the economy continued to expand. During the 1960s there emerged a new conservative viewpoint, and efforts were made by many in politics to loosen the control of the government on the economy and to return to a more laissez-faire economy. This issue is still being debated.

Questions:

a. Did the thirteen original colonies want a strong central government? Explain.

b. Why was a new Constitution necessary a few years after the end of the Revolution?

c. What role does the government have in the economy in a laissez-faire economy?

d. How did the Civil War enable the government to expand its power over the economy?

e. Between the Civil War and the Great Depression, which side, big business or organized labor (workers), did the government usually take whenever there were conflicts?

f. What programs did the Roosevelt administration carry out in response to the Great Depression?

Follow-up: Discuss your answers with your teacher.

2. Rhetorical Cues

Read the following sentences, which contain rhetorical cues to help you follow the organization of the lecture. Decide in which order you will hear them. Number them from first (1) to seventh (7).

_____ **a.** In truth, because the United States is not a pure capitalistic system, government today does not maintain a completely laissez-faire attitude toward business.

_____ **b.** The first reason the government tries to regulate the economy is to protect the environment.

_____ **c.** Let me begin today by saying that the American economy is basically a capitalistic economy. One of the important characteristics of American-style capitalism is individual ownership of property.

_____ **d.** The last reason for the government's interfering with the economy is to maintain economic stability.

_____ **e.** The second characteristic is free enterprise.

_____ **f.** The second reason the government interferes with the economy is to help people who for some reason beyond their control earn little or no income.

_____ **g.** The third characteristic is free competitive markets.

Follow-up: Check your answers with your teacher.

II. LISTENING

🎧 A. First Listening

In the introduction the lecturer discusses how a *pure* capitalist government would function in order to point out how the United States is *not* a pure capitalist country, and then he goes on to explain *why* the government interferes. Notice that the lecturer starts out with the simpler reasons and finishes with the most complex. Take down as many relevant details as possible, but be sure to take down subtopics. Continue to work on structuring your notes and using abbreviations and symbols.

NOTES

Introduction:

ST1 _____

ST2 _____

ST3 _____

ST4 _____

Follow-up: Check your major subtopics with your teacher before you listen to the lecture for the second time.

B. Further Listening

While listening again, write down necessary relevant details below the main subtopics to which they belong. Remember to structure your notes to make them easier to use later.

Follow-up: Check your notes. If you missed important information or have doubts about your notes, (1) verify them by asking a classmate questions to fill the gaps in your notes or (2) listen to the lecture a third time. When verifying your notes with a classmate, do not show each other your notes; ask specific questions to get the information you need.

Examples:
- How does the government try to help people who don't have enough money? I couldn't catch the names of the programs. Do you have them?
- Did you get why the government lowers the interest rate?

This is also a good time to check to see if the lecturer answered your *Predictions* questions about the lecture.

III. POSTLISTENING

A. Accuracy Check

Listen to the following questions, and write *short answers*. You will hear each question one time only.

1. _____
2. _____
3. _____
4. _____
5. _____
6. _____
7. _____
8. _____
9. _____
10. _____

Follow-up: Check your answers with your teacher. If your score is less than 70 percent, you may need to listen to the lecture again or rewrite your notes so that you can understand and use them later.

B. Oral Activities

1. Review

In small groups, review your notes, section by section, to be sure that all members have a complete set of notes for each subsection. At the end of this activity, your instructor will ask various class members to reproduce sections of the lecture for the whole class to listen to. At that time, check what you hear against your notes. If you don't understand or you disagree with what you hear, wait until the speaker finishes. Then bring your notes into agreement by seeking clarification, as follows:

- Excuse me, I didn't catch what you said about free enterprise.

- You said that raising taxes raises the inflation rate. I think it lowers it.

2. Transfer

If you and your classmates come from different countries, discuss these questions with a partner or in small groups. If not, discuss them with the whole class.

- Is your government basically laissez-faire, or does it take an active role in the economy?

- Does your government provide welfare, that is, help people who do not have enough money?

- Does your government provide medical care, or must people pay for it?

- Does your government regulate businesses in order to protect the environment?

C. Collaboration: Summary

In pairs, write a one-paragraph summary of the lecture. Include the main ideas from each of the main subtopics. Include important secondary points, but do not exceed 125 words.

Follow-up: Exchange summaries with at least one other pair. Find two things you like about the other summary.

D. Pursuing the Topic

The following is recommended for a closer look at the role of government in the United States:

Books/Periodicals/Internet

Galbraith, John Kennneth. *The Good Society: The Humane Agenda.* Houghton Mifflin Company, 1996.

Canadian-born U.S. economist discusses many aspects of the economy with a chapter on regulation.

Interview

Interview a U.S. citizen to find out his or her views on some of the issues highlighted in the lecture. Beforehand, write questions as a class to ask

- what the person thinks is the primary responsibility of government

- what the person thinks about tax money in the form of welfare going to unemployed healthy adults

- whether he or she thinks the government is doing enough to protect the environment

- any other questions your class is interested in

Write down the answers to the questions, and share the information with your classmates.

Variation: Invite an American to visit your class, and have the whole class interview him or her using the questions that you wrote.

Government by Constitution:
Separation of Powers/Checks and Balances

I. PRELISTENING

A. Discussion

Discuss the following questions with your classmates:

- In which of these building does the president of the United States live?

- Which building houses the meeting chambers of the House of Representatives and the Senate?

- Which of these buildings is the highest court in the United States?

- Who makes the laws in your country?

- If people in your country feel a law is unfair or unjust, what do they do?

B. Vocabulary and Key Concepts

Read through the sentences, trying to imagine which words would fit in the blanks. Then listen to a dictation of the full sentences, and write the missing words in the blanks.

1. Two important principles of the United States Constitution are

   the _____ of powers and the system of

   _____ and _____.

2. The Constitution provides for three _____

   of government: the _____, the executive,

   and the _____.

3. The legislative branch is primarily responsible for

   _____, or making, new laws. The executive

   branch executes laws by signing them and by seeing that they are

   _____.

4. The judicial branch deals with those who are

   _____ _____

   _____ a law or who are involved in a

   _____ _____.

5. The judicial branch also handles _____

   and reviews existing laws to make sure they are

   _____ _____ the

   U.S. Constitution.

6. Each branch has its specific _____

   and its own particular power, which it must not

   _____ .

7. The presidential _____

   _____ _____ is an

   obvious example of checks and balances.

8. Because it's difficult for Congress to _____

   a presidential veto, the veto may _____

   _____ _____

   _____ this new law forever.

9. Although President Nixon was _____ of

   illegal activities, he was never removed from office by Congress

   because he _____ .

10. By finding laws against abortion _____ ,

    the Supreme Court in effect made abortion

    _____ .

11. In the area of _____

    _____ , the Supreme Court declared it

    illegal to practice _____

    _____ in any form.

12. Probably the most important effect of this change was the

    _____ of public schools.

13. After the president _____

_____ _____ for the

Supreme Court, the Congress must _____

his choice.

14. Because there are only nine Supreme Court Justices, one new

Justice can change the _____

_____ _____ on the

Court itself.

Follow-up: Check the spelling of the dictated words with your teacher. Discuss the meanings of these words and any other unfamiliar words in the sentences.

C. Predictions

Using the photograph and the vocabulary exercise as a starting point, write three questions that you think will be answered in the lecture.

Example: • Which branch of government is the president part of?

1. _____

_____

2. _____

_____

3. _____

_____

Follow-up: After you have written your questions, share them with your teacher and your classmates.

D. Notetaking Preparation

1. Prelecture Reading

As we mentioned in the previous lesson, U.S. university students most often prepare for each class by reading a text chapter, an article, or even a case study. This preparation makes the instructor's lecture, usually on a topic related to the reading, easier to follow and to take notes on.

Before listening to the lecture, read the following passage carefully and answer the comprehension questions. You will notice how this preparation will aid your comprehension of the lecture.

Judicial Review

Judicial review is the power of a court to invalidate or overturn any law passed by the legislature that the court believes to be unconstitutional. The concept of judicial review as exercised by the Supreme Court of the United States is almost unique in the world. It can be called an American invention. Nowhere else does the judiciary of a country exercise final say over laws passed by the legislature. This enormous power of judicial review by the Supreme Court was established in a famous case several years after the Constitution was written, *Marbury v. Madison* (1803). The Court's opinion stated that the Constitution was superior to any acts by the legislature and that it was the Court's duty to void any laws that went against the Constitution. This power was not explicitly expressed in the Constitution, and even today, almost 200 years later, the Supreme Court's power to void laws passed by the legislature is still controversial.

If we compare judicial review in the United States with that in a few other countries, we will see just how unusual it is. In Great Britain, the right of Parliament (the legislature) to make any law it wants to cannot be challenged by the courts. The courts can *interpret* but not determine the validity of a law. In Germany, the judiciary actually has had such power since shortly after World War II, but it has been slow to exercise judicial review for cultural and historical reasons. The judiciary in Canada has had this power since 1982, but whether it will exercise it in a way similar to that exercised by the U.S. Supreme Court cannot be known yet.

Questions:

a. What is judicial review?

b. Is judicial review guaranteed by the U.S. Constitution? Explain.

c. Which of the following countries has no provisions for judicial review—Britain, Canada, or Germany?

d. Do Germany and Canada exercise judicial review more or less frequently than the United States does? Explain.

Follow-up: Check your answers with your teacher before you continue.

2. Practicing the Language of Political Science

The following exercise will help you learn language used when discussing the separate powers that each branch of the U.S. government has and the *checks and balances* that each branch has over the other two branches. Look over the schematic, which shows *some* of the powers that each branch has and how some of these powers specifically limit the powers of the other two branches. Then answer the questions that follow the schematic.

The U.S. Government

Executive Branch

- Sends suggestions to Congress (i.e., proposes new legislation)
- May veto bills sent by Congress for signature
- Nominates judges
- Makes treaties with other countries
- Prepares federal budget

Legislative Branch

- Approves federal budget
- Approves treaties
- Sends bills it has passed to president for signature
- May override veto by 2/3 majority
- Must approve appointment of judges
- May impeach the president
- May impeach judges

Judicial Branch

- Interprets laws
- May declare a law unconstitutional
- Interprets treaties

Work with a partner to answer these questions:

a. Which powers in each branch are checked by another branch?

b. Which powers seem to have no checks against them?

Follow-up: Check your answers with your classmates.

II. LISTENING

A. First Listening

The lecturer begins with a brief discussion of the Constitution of the United States and tells you its two guiding principles. She then announces her first subtopic, the three branches of the U.S. government. She goes on to explain the two guiding principles. Finally, she expands on the second principle with several examples and illustrations. (You will need to use the notetaking skills that you have learned so far to organize your notes below.)

Notes

Follow-up: Check your subtopics with your teacher. How did you organize your notes? Yours may be different from another student's. What is important is that your notes reflect the basic organization and information of the lecture.

🎧 B. Further Listening

While listening again, write down necessary relevant details below the main subtopics to which they belong.

Follow-up: Check your notes. If you missed important information or have doubts about your notes, (1) verify them by asking a classmate questions to fill the gaps in your notes or (2) listen to the lecture a third time. When verifying your notes with a classmate, do not show each other your notes; ask specific questions to get the information you need.

Examples:
- What does the judicial system do? Do you have that in your notes?
- I don't have anything in my notes about who chooses the people on the Supreme Court. Do you have it in your notes?
- What can the president do if he doesn't like a law that the Congress sends him to sign? I didn't catch that word.

This is also a good time to check to see if the lecturer answered your *Predictions* questions about the lecture.

III. POSTLISTENING

🎧 A. Accuracy Check

Listen to the following questions, and write *short answers*. You will hear each question one time only.

1. _____
2. _____
3. _____
4. _____
5. _____
6. _____
7. _____
8. _____

9. _____

10. _____

Follow-up: Check your answers with your teacher. If your score is less than 70 percent, you may need to listen to the lecture again or rewrite your notes so that you can understand and use them later.

B. Oral Activities

1. Review

In small groups, discuss your notes, section by section, to be sure that all members have a complete set of notes for each subsection. At the end of this activity, your instructor will ask various class members to reproduce sections of the lecture for the whole class to listen to. At that time, check what you hear against your notes. If you don't understand or you disagree with what you hear, wait until the speaker finishes. Then bring your notes into agreement by seeking clarification, as follows:

- Did you say that Congress can veto a law? My notes say that the president can veto a law.

- Excuse me, could you repeat what you said about Watergate?

2. Transfer

If you and your classmates come from different countries, discuss these questions with a partner or in small groups. If not, discuss them with the whole class.

- How is the power to make and enforce laws in your country divided? Explain.

- Can a law be overturned by the judicial branch in your country? If so, under what circumstances?

- Do you think the legislative branch of a government should have the power to remove the president of a country from office?

C. Collaboration: Writing Answers to Essay Questions

To help you prepare for the essay questions in the Unit Quiz at the end of this unit, plan and write essay answers to the following questions on the Constitution and the separation of powers. Work in groups of three or four. Appoint one member of the group to do the actual writing; all members of the group should participate in planning and helping with the answers.

Questions:

1. List the three branches of the U.S. government and describe their primary duties.

2. What are the two guiding principles of the U.S. Constitution, and what is their purpose?

Follow-up: Share your answers with at least one other group that has written on the same question(s). Or share your answers orally with the class, and discuss the strengths in each answer.

D. Pursuing the Topic

The following are recommended for a closer look at issues related to the Constitution of the United States:

Books/Periodicals/Internet

TIME, July 6, 1987.
> *This issue commemorates the 200th anniversary of the American Constitution. Numerous articles and essays discuss various aspects of and issues involved with the Constitution, among them its history and impact, landmark Supreme Court decisions, and current issues.*

Do an Internet search, using the keyword *U.S. Constitution*, to find a multitude of sites that offer the text and an analysis of the U.S. Constitution.

Films/Videos

All the President's Men, Alan J. Pakula, director; 138 minutes, PG.
> *This film is based on the true story of two investigative reporters who broke the story of the Watergate scandal, which eventually brought down the Nixon administration.*

Common Law and the Jury System

I. PRELISTENING

A. Discussion

Discuss the following questions with your classmates:

- Have you seen scenes of American courtrooms in movies or on TV?

- Do you think they realistically depict what happens in courtrooms?

- How are courtrooms different in your country?

B. Vocabulary and Key Concepts

Read through the sentences, trying to imagine which words would fit in the blanks. Then listen to a dictation of the full sentences, and write the missing words in the blanks.

1. The average person in the legal profession would probably say it's better to let a dozen _____ people go free than to punish one innocent person _____.

2. The guiding principle for the U.S. legal system is that an accused person is _____

   _____ _____

   _____.

3. Under civil law the judge consults a complex

   _____ _____

   _____ to decide whether the defendant is guilty and, if so, what sentence to give.

4. Under _____ _____ the judge considers the _____ set by other court decisions.

5. The jury hears _____ in either civil or criminal trials and reaches a _____.

6. A civil trial is one that deals with disputes between

   _____ _____, often involving contracts or property rights.

7. In a civil trial, the jury decides which side is right and how much money should be paid in _____ and _____ _____.

8. For a jury to convict a person in a criminal case, they must believe the person guilty _____ _____ _____ _____.

9. A person's liberty and even life can be taken away if he or she is _____, that is, found guilty, of a crime.

10. Some of a judge's responsibilities are excluding _____ remarks and questions by lawyers and witnesses and deciding what kind of _____ is _____.

11. If the required number of jurors cannot agree on a decision, it is called a _____ jury, and the law requires a new trial.

12. What happens in plea bargaining is that the accused _____ _____ to a _____ _____.

Follow-up: Check the spelling of the dictated words with your teacher. Discuss the meanings of these words and any other unfamiliar words in the sentences.

C. Predictions

Using the photograph and the vocabulary exercise as a starting point, write three questions that you think will be answered in the lecture.

Example: • How many people are on a jury?

1. _____

_____

2. _____

_____

3. _____

_____

Follow-up: After you have written your questions, share them with your teacher and your classmates.

D. Notetaking Preparation

1. Prelecture Reading

Before listening to a rather difficult lecture on the U.S. legal system, read a related passage dealing with *precedents* and surrogate motherhood, and then answer the comprehension questions that follow. Although somewhat difficult, the reading and the questions will prepare you for the lecture you will hear later.

The Baby M Case

The Baby M case became a controversial legal case in the United States in 1988. At issue were Baby M's custody and the validity of a contract. The contract provided that a woman, the surrogate mother, would have a baby for an infertile couple by artificial insemination of the husband's sperm and would receive payment for this service. Certainly, Baby M was not the first baby born to a surrogate mother, but in this case the surrogate mother, Mary Beth Whitehead-Gould, changed her mind after the baby was born and did not want to give the baby up, as she had agreed to do in the contract. The Sterns, the couple who had contracted for the baby, insisted that Ms. Whitehead-Gould fulfill the terms of the contract, and they took her to court. The New Jersey Supreme Court ruled that this type of contract was against public policy (the good of the general public) and, therefore, could not be enforced. (However, the court did award *custody* of the baby to the biological father. The mother, Ms. Whitehead-Gould, was awarded limited visitation rights.) This particular ruling was very important because there had been no previous court decision of this type at the level of a state supreme court. Therefore, this decision establishes a precedent for other states when they have to deal with the issue of surrogacy.

Questions:

a. Are Baby M's natural mother and father married to each other?

b. Who wanted to break the contract, Mary Beth Whitehead-Gould or the Sterns?

c. In this reading, *precedent* most nearly means
   1. a reason not to do something
   2. a decision used as a standard
   3. proof of innocence
   4. proof of guilt

d. Was there a precedent for judging surrogacy contracts before the Baby M case?

e. In what sense will the Baby M case serve as a precedent in the future?

Follow-up: Discuss your answers with your teacher before you continue.

2. Courtroom Language

Look at the following illustration of a typical courtroom scene. Work with a partner to answer the following questions.

a. Who keeps a written record of what is said in court?

b. Who ensures that the trial is conducted according to the law?

c. Who is a person who has knowledge of the case and is called to testify in court?

d. Who deliberates on the facts of the case and delivers a verdict (decision)?

e. Who has custody of prisoners and maintains order in the court?

f. Who is the person against whom the court action has been taken?

g. Who initiates court action against the defendant?

h. Who takes care of records involved in the court case?

Follow-up: Check your answers with your teacher.

II. LISTENING

A. First Listening

The lecturer begins with a rather long introduction in which she attempts to provide some background to a rather technical discussion of the U.S. legal system, which is based on common law. She then goes on to discuss the jury system and, finally, plea bargaining. It is not necessary to take notes until she begins to compare common law to civil law. Use the notetaking skills that you have practiced to make a set of meaningful and usable notes.

NOTES

Follow-up: Check your subtopics with your teacher. How did you organize your notes? Yours may be different from another student's. What is important is that your notes should reflect the basic organization and information of the lecture.

🎧 B. Further Listening

While listening again, write down necessary relevant details below the main subtopics to which they belong.

Follow-up: Check your notes. If you missed important information or have doubts about your notes, (1) verify them by asking a classmate questions to fill the gaps in your notes or (2) listen to the lecture a third time. When verifying your notes with a classmate, do not show each other your notes; ask specific questions to get the information you need.

Examples:
- What is the difference between common law and civil law? Do you have that in your notes?
- I don't have anything in my notes about what a judge does. Do you have it in your notes?

This is also a good time to check to see if the lecturer answered your *Predictions* questions about the lecture.

III. POSTLISTENING

🎧 A. Accuracy Check

Listen to the following questions, and write *short answers*. You will hear each question one time only.

1. _____

2. _____

3. _____

4. _____

5. _____

6. _____

7. _____

8. _____

9. _____

10. _____

Follow-up: Check your answers with your teacher. If your score is less than 70 percent, you may need to listen to the lecture again or rewrite your notes so that you can understand and use them later.

B. Oral Activities

1. Review

In small groups, discuss your notes, section by section, to be sure that all members have a complete set of notes for each subsection. At the end of this activity, your instructor will ask various class members to reproduce sections of the lecture for the whole class to listen to. At that time, check what you hear against your notes. If you don't understand or you disagree with what you hear, wait until the speaker finishes. Then bring your notes into agreement by seeking clarification, as follows:

- Would you please repeat what you said about a written code of laws?

- Excuse me, but you didn't mention plea bargaining. I think it's important.

2. Transfer

If your class is multinational, prepare a short oral report about the legal system of your country, comparing and contrasting it to the legal system of the United States. Work with other students from your country.

If your classmates are all from your country, discuss the similarities and differences as a class.

C. Collaboration: Discussion

Discuss these questions in small groups. Appoint one person to report your group's responses for each question to the class.

1. Which system do you think results in more convictions, or guilty verdicts, and why: civil law as practiced in Europe or common law as practiced in Great Britain and the United States?

2. Compare the advantages of having a judge decide a case without a jury to the advantages of having a jury decide a case.

3. Which principle of law do you think is fairer, "innocent until proven guilty" or "guilty until proven innocent"? Why?

D. Pursuing the Topic

The following are recommended for a closer look at the justice system in the United States:

Books/Periodicals/Internet

Posner, Richard A. "Juries on Trial." *Commentary*, March 1995, pp. 49–53.
> *Posner discusses criticism of the American jury system by experts who claim that the system is too easy on the defendants in criminal cases and too sympathetic to plaintiffs in civil cases. Recent books suggest that the jury system is likely to end in civil cases.*

www.uscourts.gov
> *Explore this Web site to find out more about the judicial branch of the U.S. government.*

www.crimelibrary.com
> *This Web site contains a wealth of information about notorious and highly publicized crimes and criminals.*

Films/Videos

The Verdict, Sidney Lumet, director; 129 minutes, R.
> *This film depicts courtroom drama as a down-and-out Boston lawyer takes on a medical malpractice suit.*

Reversal of Fortune, Barbet Schroeder, director; 120 minutes, R.
> *A Harvard law professor and lawyer attempts to reverse the conviction of a man found guilty of the attempted murder of his wife in this film, which is based on a true story.*

Field Trip

If you are studying in the United States, it may be possible for your instructor to make arrangements for your class to visit a local courthouse, where you can watch the proceedings. Virtually all courtroom proceedings are open to the public.

Now that you have completed the chapters in this unit, your teacher may want you to take a quiz. Your teacher will tell you whether or not you can use your notes to answer the questions on the quiz. If you can use your notes, review them before taking the quiz so that you can anticipate the questions and know where to find the answers. If you cannot use your notes, *study them carefully before you take the quiz*, concentrating on organizing the information into main ideas and details that support these main ideas.

Work in small groups to help each other anticipate the questions your teacher will ask. Before breaking up into groups, review your notes and highlight important, noteworthy points. After reviewing your notes, break up into groups. Discuss and write specific short-answer questions and more general essay questions. (For guidelines in writing questions, see the Unit Quiz Directions at the end of Unit 1.)

Write your group's questions on the following pages.

Unit Five The Official Side

Chapter 13 The Role of Government in the Economy

Assign one group member to write down the questions; all members will help plan and compose the questions. For the lecture on the role of government in the economy, write five short-answer questions that can be answered with a few words or one or two sentences. In addition, write two essay questions; word the questions so that they can easily be turned into topic sentences.

Short-Answer Questions

1. _____

   _____

2. _____

   _____

3. _____

   _____

4. _____

   _____

5. _____

   _____

Essay Questions

1. _____

   _____

2. _____

   _____

Follow-up: Write your questions on the board to discuss as a class.

Written Follow-up: Prepare for the quiz by writing answers to the questions your class has proposed. You may have abbreviations in your notes, but do not use abbreviations other than standard ones like *U.S.* in your answers.

UNIT QUIZ PREPARATION

Chapter 14 Government by Constitution: Separation of Powers/Checks and Balances

Assign one group member to write down the questions; all members will help plan and compose the questions. For the lecture on government by constitution, write five short-answer questions that can be answered with a few words or one or two sentences. In addition, write two essay questions; word the questions so that they can easily be turned into topic sentences.

Short-Answer Questions

1. _____

_____

2. _____

_____

3. _____

_____

4. _____

_____

5. _____

_____

Essay Questions

1. _____

_____

2. _____

_____

Follow-up: Write your questions on the board to discuss as a class.

Written Follow-up: Prepare for the quiz by writing answers to the questions your class has proposed. You may have abbreviations in your notes, but do not use abbreviations other than standard ones like *U.S.* in your answers.

UNIT QUIZ PREPARATION

Chapter 15 Common Law and the Jury System

Assign one group member to write down the questions; all members will help plan and compose the questions. For the lecture on common law and the jury system, write five short-answer questions that can be answered with a few words or one or two sentences. In addition, write two essay questions; word the questions so that they can easily be turned into topic sentences.

Short-Answer Questions

1. _____

   _____

2. _____

   _____

3. _____

   _____

4. _____

   _____

5. _____

   _____

Essay Questions

1. _____

   _____

2. _____

   _____

Follow-up: Write your questions on the board to discuss as a class.

Written Follow-up: Prepare for the quiz by writing answers to the questions your class has proposed. You may have abbreviations in your notes, but do not use abbreviations other than standard ones like *U.S.* in your answers.

Appendices

Unit One | **The Face of the People**

Chapter 1   The Population

I. PRELISTENING

B. Vocabulary and Key Concepts

1. Most countries take a <u>census</u> every ten years or so in order to count the people and to know where they are living.

2. A country with a growing population is a country that is becoming more <u>populous</u>.

3. A person's <u>race</u> is partly determined by skin color and type of hair as well as other physical characteristics.

4. The majority of the U.S. population is of European <u>origin</u>.

5. The <u>geographical</u> <u>distribution</u> of a country's population gives information about where the people are living.

6. The total population of the United States is <u>made</u> <u>up</u> <u>of</u> many different kinds of people.

7. In other words, the population <u>comprises</u> people of different races and ages.

8. The average age of the U.S. population, which is a <u>relatively</u> large one, has been getting <u>progressively</u> higher recently.

9. <u>Metropolitan</u> areas are more <u>densely</u> populated than rural areas. That is, they have more people per square mile.

10. The use of antibiotics has greatly <u>decreased</u> the <u>death</u> <u>rate</u> throughout much of the world.

11. A country whose <u>birth</u> <u>rate</u> is higher than its death rate will have an <u>increasing</u> population.

12. On the average, women have a higher <u>life</u> <u>expectancy</u> than men do.

D. Notetaking Preparation

1. Number Notation

a. 18.5 million
b. 80 percent
c. one half
d. 13.4 million
e. two out of ten

f. four percent
g. nineteen ninety
h. 40 percent
i. three quarters
j. 33.1 percent

LECTURE: Population

Today we're going to talk about population in the United States. According to the most recent government census, the population is 281,421,906 people. This represents an increase of almost 33 million people since the 1990 census. A population of over 281 million makes the United States the third most populous country in the whole world. As you probably know, the People's Republic of China is the most populous country in the world. Do you know which is the second most populous? If you thought India, you were right. The fourth, fifth, and sixth most populous countries are Indonesia, Brazil, and Pakistan. Now let's get back to the United States. Let's look at the total U.S. population figure of 281 million in three different ways. The first way is by race and origin; the second is by geographical distribution, or by where people live; and the third way is by the age and sex of the population.

First of all, let's take a look at the population by race and origin. The latest U.S. census reports that 75.1 percent of the population is white, whereas 12.3 percent is black. Three percent are of Asian origin, and 1 percent is Native American. 2.4 percent of the population is a mixture of two or more races, and 5.5 percent report themselves as "of some other race." Let's make sure your figures are right: white, 75.1 percent; black, 12.3 percent; Asian, 3 percent; Native American, 1 percent; a mixture of two or more races, 2.4 percent; and of some other race, 5.5 percent. Hispanics, whose origins lie in Spanish-speaking countries, comprise whites, blacks, and Native Americans, so they are already included in the above figures. It is important to note that Hispanics make up 12.5 percent of the present U.S. population, however. Finally, the census tells us that 31 million people in the United States were born in another country. Of the 31 million foreign born, the largest part, 27.6 percent are from Mexico. The next largest group, from the Philippines, number 4.3 percent.

Another way of looking at the population is by geographical distribution. Do you have any idea which states are the five most populous in the United States? Well, I'll help you out there. The five most populous states, with population figures, are California, with almost 34 million; New York, with 21 million; Texas, with 19 million; Florida, with 16 million; and Illinois with 12.5 million people. Did you get all those figures down? If not, I'll give you a chance later to check your figures. Well, then, let's move on. All told, over half, or some 58 percent of the population, lives in the South and in the West of the United States. This figure, 58 percent, is surprising to many people. It is surprising because the East is more densely populated. Nevertheless, there are more people all together in the South and West. To understand this seeming contradiction, one need only consider the relatively larger size of many southern and western states, so although there are more people, they are distributed over a larger area. To finish up this section on geographical distribution, consider that more than three- quarters of the people live in metropolitan areas like Los Angeles, New York, Chicago, and Houston. That means that only 20 percent, or 2 out of 10 people, live in rural areas. An interesting side note is that some 3,800,000 U.S. citizens live abroad, that is, in foreign countries.

Before we finish today, I want to discuss the distribution of the U.S. population in terms of age and sex. Just for interest, would you say there are more men or more women in the United States? (pause) Well, according to the 2000 census, there are more women. In fact, there are more than five million more women than men in the U.S. population. If we consider that more males than females are born each year, how can this difference be explained? Well, for a variety of complicated reasons that we can't go into here, there is a progressively higher death rate for males as they get older. This is seen in 2003 life expectancy figures: the life expectancy for women is 80.4 years whereas for men it is only 74.5 years. I don't know how these life expectancy figures compare to those in your countries, but statistically women generally live longer than men worldwide. Now, to finish up, let's look at the average age of the whole population. Overall, the average age of the population is increasing: from 33.1 years in 1990 to 35.3 years in 2000. The average age has been slowly, but steadily, increasing over the past several decades. This trend toward a higher average age can be explained by a decreasing birth rate and an increasing life expectancy for the population as a whole. I'd like to investigate these two subjects further, but I see our time is up, so we'll have to call it quits for today. You may want to pursue the topic of the aging U.S. population further, so there are some suggestions at the end of the lesson to help you do so.

III. POSTLISTENING

A. Accuracy Check

[Leave pauses between questions to give time for students to write answers.]

1. Which two countries have a larger population than the United States?

2. What was the population of the United States in the latest census?

3. Which group is bigger, blacks or Hispanics?

4. Which state is more populous, Florida or Texas?

5. In what two regions of the country do most Americans live?

6. What percentage of the population lives in rural areas?

7. How many more women than men are there in the U.S. population?

8. About how many years longer do women live than men in the United States?

9. What was the increase in the average age from 1990 to 2000?

10. What two factors account for the increase in the average age?

Chapter 2   Immigration: Past and Present

I. PRELISTENING

B. Vocabulary and Key Concepts

1. Throughout history, people have moved, or <u>immigrated,</u> to new countries to live.

2. <u>Natural</u> <u>disasters</u> can take many forms: those that are characterized by a shortage of rain or food are called <u>droughts</u> and <u>famines,</u> respectively.

3. Sometimes people immigrate to a new country to escape political or religious <u>persecution</u>.

4. Rather than immigrants, the early <u>settlers</u> from Great Britain considered themselves <u>colonists</u>; they had left home to settle new land for the mother country.

5. The so-called Great Immigration, which can be divided into three <u>stages</u>, or time periods, began about 1830 and lasted till about 1930.

6. The Industrial Revolution, which began in the nineteenth century, caused <u>widespread</u> <u>unemployment</u> as machines replaced workers.

7. The <u>scarcity</u> of farmland in Europe caused many people to immigrate to the United States, where farmland was more abundant.

8. Land in the United States was plentiful and available when the country was <u>expanding</u> westward. In fact, the U.S. government offered free public land to <u>citizens</u> in 1862.

9. The <u>failure</u> of the Irish potato crop in the middle of the nineteenth century caused widespread starvation.

10. The Great Depression of the 1930s and World War II contributed to the noticeable <u>decrease</u> in immigration after 1930.

11. The first law that <u>limited</u> the number of immigrants coming from a certain part of the world was the Chinese Exclusion Act of 1882.

12. It is important to note that in 1965 strict <u>quotas</u> based on nationality were eliminated.

13. At the end of the 1940s, immigration began to increase again and has, in general, risen <u>steadily</u> since then.

14. Will the <u>trend</u> continue for non-Europeans to immigrate to the United States?

15. The U.S. immigration laws of today in general require that new immigrants have the <u>skills</u> necessary to succeed in the United States because industry no longer requires large numbers of <u>unskilled</u> workers.

D. Notetaking Preparation

1. Dates: Teens and Tens

a. 1850   **f.** 1776

b. 1915   **g.** 1882

c. the 1840s   **h.** 1929

d. from 1890 to 1930   **i.** 1860

e. between 1750 and 1850   **j.** from approximately
                                    1830 to 1930

II. LISTENING

LECTURE: Immigration: Past and Present

The act of immigrating, or coming to a new country to live, is certainly nothing new. Throughout history, people have immigrated, or moved to new countries, for many different reasons. Sometimes these reasons were economic or political. Other people moved because of natural disasters such as droughts or famines. And some people moved to escape religious or political persecution. No matter what the reason, most people do not want to leave their native land and do so only under great pressure of some sort, but a few people seem quite adventuresome and restless by nature and like to move a lot. It seems both kinds of people came to America to live. The subject of immigration is quite fascinating to most Americans, as they view themselves as a nation of immigrants. However, the early Britons who came to what is today the United States considered themselves "settlers" or "colonists," rather than immigrants. These people did not exactly think they were moving to a new country but were merely settling new land for the "mother country." There were also large numbers of Dutch, French, German, and Scotch-Irish settlers, as well as large numbers of blacks brought from Africa as slaves. At the time of independence from Britain in 1776, about 40 percent of people living in what is now the United States were non-British. The majority of people, however, spoke English, and the traditions that formed the basis of life were mainly British traditions. This period we have just been discussing is usually referred to as the Colonial Period. Today, we're a little more interested in actual immigration after this period. Let's first look at what is often called the Great Immigration, which began about 1830 and ended in 1930. Then let's consider the reasons for this so-called Great Immigration and the reasons it ended. Finally, let's talk about the immigration situation in the United States today.

As I said, we'll begin our discussion today with the period of history called the Great Immigration, which lasted from approximately 1830 to 1930. It will be easier if we look at the Great Immigration in terms of three major stages, or time periods. The first stage was from approximately 1830 to 1860. Before this time, the number of immigrants coming to the United States was comparatively small, only about 10,000 a year. However, the rate began to climb in the 1830s when about 600,000 immigrants arrived. The rate continued to climb during the 1840s with a total of 1,700,000 people arriving in that decade. The rate continued to climb, and during the 1850s 2,600,000 immigrants arrived. During this first stage of the Great Immigration, that is, between the years 1830 and 1860, the majority of immigrants came from Germany, Great Britain, and Ireland. Now let's consider the second stage of the Great Immigration. The second stage was from 1860 to 1890, during which time another 10,000,000 people arrived. Between 1860 and 1890 the majority of immigrants continued to be from Germany, Ireland, and Great Britain. However, during the second stage, a smaller, but significant, number of immigrants came from the Scandinavian nations of Denmark, Norway, and Sweden. The third stage of the Great Immigration, which lasted from 1890 to 1930, was the era of heaviest immigration. Between the years 1890 and 1930, almost 22 million immigrants arrived in the United States. Most of these new arrivals came from the Southern European countries of Greece, Italy, Portugal, and Spain and the Eastern European countries of Poland and Russia.

Now that we know something about the numbers and origins of immigrants who came to the States during the Great Immigration, let's consider the reasons why most of these people immigrated to the United States. Why did such large numbers of Europeans leave their homes for life in an unknown country? It would be impossible to discuss all the complex political and economic reasons in any depth today, but we can touch on a few interesting facts that might help to clarify the situation for you. First of all, one of the most important reasons was that the population of Europe doubled between the years 1750 and 1850. At the same time that the population was growing so rapidly, the Industrial Revolution in Europe was causing widespread unemployment. The combination of increased population and the demand for land by industry also meant that farmland was becoming increasingly scarce in Europe. The scarcity of farmland in Europe meant that the abundance of available land in the growing country of the United States was a great attraction. During these years, the United States was an expanding country, and it seemed that there was no end to land. In fact, in 1862 the government offered public land free to citizens and to immigrants who were planning to become citizens. In addition to available farmland, there were also plentiful jobs during these years of great economic growth. Other attractions were freedom from religious or political persecution. Some other groups also came to the United States as the direct results of natural disasters that left them in desperate situations. For example, the frequent failure of the potato crop in Ireland between the years 1845 and 1849 led to widespread starvation in that country, and people were driven to immigrate. Another factor that affected the number of immigrants coming to the United States was improved ocean transport beginning in the 1840s. At that time, ships large enough to carry large numbers of people began to make regular trips across the ocean. Now let's summarize the reasons for the high rate of immigration to the United States during the years we discussed: first, the doubling of the population in Europe between 1750 and 1850; second, the unemployment caused by the Industrial Revolution; and third, the land scarcity in Europe, followed by religious and political persecution and natural disaster. These reasons combined with improved transportation probably account for the largest number of immigrants.

I would now like to talk briefly about the period of time following the Great Immigration and the reasons for the decline in the rate of immigration. Although immigration continues today, immigration numbers have never again reached the levels that we discussed previously. There are several reasons for this decline. This decline was in part due to various laws whose aim was to limit the number of immigrants coming from different parts of the world to the United States. The first such law that limited the number of immigrants coming from a certain part of the world was the Chinese Exclusion Act of 1882. This law was followed by many other laws that also tried to limit the numbers of people immigrating from various countries or parts of the world. In addition to such laws, certainly economic and geopolitical events as important as the Great Depression starting in 1929 and World War II also contributed to the decline in immigration.

Let's conclude our talk by discussing the current situation with respect to immigration, which is quite different from that in the past. To understand some of the changes, it's important to note that in 1965 strict quotas based on nationality were eliminated. Let's see how different things are today from the past. As I noted, the greatest number of immigrants to the United States have historically been European. According to U.S. Census figures, in 1860, the percentage of immigrants that were European was 92 percent. But by 1960, the percentage of European immigrants had dropped to 74.5 percent, and by the year 2002, it had dropped to 14 percent! In 2002, 52.2 percent of immigrants came from Latin America, that is, from the Caribbean, Central America, and South America. Mexico is ordinarily considered part of North America, but the U.S. Census Bureau considers Mexico as a Central American country in terms of immigration statistics, and estimates that more than one-third of the total of all immigrants to the United States in 2002 came from Mexico or another Central American country. The next largest percentage, 25.5 percent, of immigrants came from Asia, mainly from the Philippines, China, and India.

Although immigration dropped sharply when the United States entered World War I and remained low throughout the Depression and World War II years, at the end of the 1940s, immigration began to increase again and has, in general, risen steadily since then. It might surprise you to know that the actual number of immigrants coming yearly to the States in recent years is about the same as the numbers coming yearly between 1900 and 1910. Keep in mind, though, that the population of the United States is much larger now than at the turn of the century, so that while the yearly numbers may be similar, the percentage of the population that is foreign-born is considerably smaller today than it was a century ago.

It might be interesting to speculate on immigration in the future. Will the trend continue for non-Europeans to immigrate to the United States? The answer is probably yes for the foreseeable future. Do these non-European people come to the United States for the same reasons that Europeans came? Well, land is no longer plentiful and cheap. Industry no longer requires large numbers of unskilled workers. In fact, the government usually tries to restrict immigration to those people who already have the skills to be successful in U.S. society. Still, people come for political and economic reasons and probably will continue to do so.

III. POSTLISTENING

A. Accuracy Check

1. What did the earliest Britons who came to what is now the United States consider themselves to be?

2. Which five non-English groups came to the United States during the Colonial Period?

3. Of the three stages of the Great Immigration, in which did the heaviest immigration occur?

4. From which two areas did most immigrants arrive between the years 1890 and 1930?

5. What three conditions in Europe caused a lot of immigration to the United States during the Great Immigration?

6. What conditions in the United States attracted early immigrants?

7. Give an example of a natural disaster that caused immigration to the United States.

8. What three reasons are given for a decline in immigration after the period of the Great Immigration?

9. How is the origin of people who immigrate to the United States today different from those who immigrated during the Great Immigration?

10. Today, why does the U.S. government try to restrict immigration to people who already have the skills to be successful?

Chapter 3   Americans at Work

I. PRELISTENING

B. Vocabulary and Key Concepts

1. As we look at the changes over the last century, we'll use a lot of <u>statistics</u> to describe these changes.

2. While the number of people in these <u>goods</u> <u>producing</u> industries went down, the number of people in the <u>service</u> industries went up.

3. Over the years, child labor laws became much <u>stricter</u> and by 1999, it was <u>illegal</u> for anyone under sixteen to work full-time in any of the fifty States.

4. In 1900 the average <u>per</u> <u>capita</u> income was $4,200.

5. One of the important <u>benefits</u> most workers received later in the century was <u>health</u> <u>insurance</u>.

6. Whereas <u>wages</u> and salaries rose over the century, the average <u>workweek</u> dropped.

7. People often tend to <u>romanticize</u> the past and talk about "the good old days."

8. According to a 2003 <u>study</u> released by the United Nations International Labor Organization, U.S. workers are the most <u>productive</u> in the world.

9. Longer working hours in the United States is a <u>rising</u> trend, while the trend in other industrialized countries is the <u>opposite</u>.

10. Workers in some European countries actually <u>outproduce</u> American workers per hour of work.

11. This higher rate of productivity might be because European workers are less <u>stressed</u> than U.S. workers.

12. Between 1949 and 1974, increases in productivity were <u>matched</u> by increases in wages.

13. After 1974, productivity increased in manufacturing and services, but real wages <u>stagnated</u>.

14. The money goes for salaries to <u>CEOs</u>, to the stock market, and to corporate <u>profits</u>.

15. Some people say that labor <u>unions</u> have lost power since the beginning of the 1980s, and that the government has passed laws that <u>favor</u> the rich and weaken the rights of the workers.

II. LISTENING

LECTURE: Americans at Work

Whether you love it or hate it, work is a major part of most people's lives everywhere in the world. Americans are no exception. Americans might complain about "blue Monday," when they have to go back to work after the weekend, but most people put a lot of importance on their job, not only in terms of money but also in terms of identity. In fact, when Americans are introduced to a new person, they almost always ask each other, "What do you do?" They are asking, what is your job or profession. Today, however, we won't look at work in terms of what work means socially or psychologically. Rather, we're going to take a look at work in the United States today from two perspectives. First, we'll take a historical look at work in America. We'll do that by looking at how things changed for the American worker from the beginning to the end of the twentieth century, that is, from the year 1900 to the year 1999. Then we'll look at how U.S. workers are doing today.

As we look at the changes over the last century, we're going to use a lot of statistics to describe these changes. You will need to write down a lot of numbers in today's lecture. First, let's consider how the type of work people were involved in changed. At the beginning of the twentieth century, about 38 percent of the workforce was involved in agriculture; that is, they worked on a farm. By the end of the century, only 3 percent still worked on farms. There was also a large decrease in the number of people working in mining, manufacturing, and construction. The number of workers in mining, manufacturing, and construction went down from 31 percent to 19 percent.

While the number of people in these goods producing industries went down, the number of people in the service industries went up. As you may know, a service industry is one that provides a service, rather than goods or products. A few examples include transportation, tourism, banking, advertising, health care, and legal services. I'm sure you can think of more. The service industry workforce jumped from 31 percent of the workforce at the turn of the century to 78 percent in 1999.

Let's recap the numbers: in 1900, 38 percent in agriculture; 31 percent in mining, manufacturing, and construction; and 31 percent in the service industries. That should add up to 100 percent. In 1999, 3 percent in agriculture; 19 percent in mining, manufacturing, and construction; and 78 percent in the service industries. Again, that should add up to 100 percent.

The labor force changed in other important ways. For example, child labor was not unusual at the beginning of the twentieth century. In 1900 there were 1,750,000 children aged ten to fifteen working full-time in the labor force. This was 6 percent of the labor force. Over the years, child labor laws became much stricter and by 1999, it was illegal for anyone under sixteen to work full-time in any of the fifty states. While the number of children in the workforce went down, the number of women went up dramatically. In 1900, only 19 percent of women were employed; in 1999, 60 percent of women were holding down jobs.

Let's see what has happened to wages and salaries. All the numbers I will give you are in terms of 1999 dollars. Let me explain. In 1900 the average per capita income was $4,200 a year. That does not mean that the average worker in 1900 earned $4,200, but that what he or she earned was equal to $4,200 in 1999. That is, the amount of money the average worker earned in 1900 was worth the same as $4,200 in 1999. The average per capita income in 1999 was $33,700. Not only did people earn a lot more money at the end of the century, they also received a lot more in benefits than at the beginning of the century. One of the important benefits most workers received later in the century was health insurance. Whereas wages and salaries rose over the century, the average workweek dropped. That is, workers, in general, did not work as long hours in 1999 as they did in 1900.

The last area that I'd like to give you a few statistics about is workplace safety. Most of us who go to work every day don't think a lot about whether we are safe or not, but in 1900 it was a real concern for a lot of workers. There aren't many statistics available, but the U.S. government does have statistics on two industries that will give you some idea of the differences today. In 1900 almost 1,500 workers were killed in coal-mining accidents; in 1999, the number was 35. 2,555 railroad workers were killed in 1900, compared to 56 in 1999.

People often tend to romanticize the past and talk about "the good old days," but I think it's fair to say that by the end of the twentieth century, U.S. workers in general made more money, they enjoyed more benefits, and their working conditions had improved greatly.

Now let's turn our attention to the current situation for U.S. workers. The picture is not so rosy as the one drawn by comparing U.S. workers at the beginning and the end of the twentieth century. I'm going to focus on the current situation in terms of productivity, working hours, and wages and salaries.

First let's consider the number of hours worked. According to a 2003 study released by the United Nations International Labor Organization, U.S. workers are the most productive in the world among industrialized nations, but they work longer hours than European workers to achieve this productivity. Europeans typically have four to six weeks of vacation a year, whereas the average American worker has only about two weeks. This study points out that the longer working hours in the United States is a rising trend, while the trend in other industrialized countries is the opposite.

Workers in some European countries actually outproduce American workers per hour of work. It has been suggested that this higher rate of productivity might be because European workers are less stressed than U.S. workers.

At any rate, there seems to be general agreement that U.S. productivity has greatly increased over the last thirty years. However, workers have not seen their wages rise at the same rate. A group of sociologists in their book *Inequality by Design* point out that there is a growing gap between rich Americans and everyone else in the United States. They write that between 1949 and 1974, increases in productivity were matched by increases in wages for workers in both manufacturing and the service industries, but since 1974 productivity increased 68 percent in manufacturing and 50 percent in services, but real wages stagnated. That is, wages moved up little or not at all. Where does all the money generated by the increased productivity go then? According to the authors of this book, the money goes for salaries to CEOs, to the stock market, and to corporate profits. Workers play a great role in increasing productivity, but no longer see their wages connected to increased productivity. In other words, CEOs' salaries, the stock market, and corporate profits go up as work productivity goes up, but workers' wages do not.

What are the reasons why U.S. workers, who are the most productive in the world, have to work longer hours, have fewer vacations days, and see their wages stagnate and not rising at the same rate as productivity? The answer to this question is complex and controversial, but there are two reasons most people who speak or write about these issues mention: The first is that labor unions in the United States have lost great power since the beginning of the 1980s, and the second is that the government has passed laws that favor the rich and weaken the rights of the workers.

I see our time is up. See you next time.

III. POSTLISTENING

A. Accuracy Check

1. What percentage of the workforce was engaged in agriculture in 1900?

2. What percentage of the workforce was still engaged in agriculture in 1999?

3. At the end of the twentieth century, which industries had the largest percentage of the workforce?

4. Compare the number of women in the workforce in 1900 and in 1999.

5. Compare the average per capita income in 1900 and in 1999.

6. What is one benefit that most U.S. workers received by the end of the twentieth century?

7. Which workers, U.S. or European workers, work longer hours?

8. What might be one reason that some European workers out produce U.S. workers per hour?

9. According to the authors of *Inequality by Design*, are wages in manufacturing and service industries increasing at the same rate as productivity?

10. Again, according to the authors of *Inequality by Design*, where does the money generated by increased productivity go?

Unit Two | # The American Character

Chapter 4   Family in the United States

I. PRELISTENING

B. Vocabulary and Key Concepts

1. A hundred years ago, one heard the same comments about the family that one hears today—in short, that the American family is <u>disintegrating</u>.

2. Proof of this disintegration included evidence that women were not completely content with their <u>domestic</u> <u>role</u>.

3. To the contrary, the very <u>nature</u> of the family has changed <u>drastically</u> in the last fifty years.

4. To be sure, the family is a very <u>sensitive</u> <u>barometer</u> for what is happening in the society.

5. Demographically, the <u>predominant</u> <u>configuration</u> of the family was the traditional one.

6. The country idealized the family in these years: there was a <u>commitment</u> to the family and a <u>reverence</u> for it.

7. Three characteristics stand out in this period: <u>conformity</u> to social norms, greater male domination of the family, and clear-cut <u>gender</u> roles.

8. These decades were characterized by a <u>lack</u> of conformity to social norms and included the sexual revolution and the women's <u>liberation</u> movement.

9. Another important movement was the drive for self-expression and <u>self-fulfillment</u>.

10. The new configuration of the family had to include families of <u>cohabiting</u> <u>couples</u>, with or without children.

11. The number of single-parent households <u>tripled</u>, and the number of unmarried couples <u>quadrupled</u>.

12. They see a continuing <u>decline</u> in divorce rates since the 1980s but also a decline in birth rates after an <u>initial</u> increase in the 1980s.

13. There is an attempt to <u>balance</u> work with family obligations, and concern seems to be shifting from <u>individualism</u> to the new familism.

14. Places of work may offer more <u>flexible</u> working hours and <u>on-site</u> day care.

15. For its part, the government could <u>mandate</u> parental leave and family <u>allowances</u>.

II. LISTENING

LECTURE: Family in the United States

A hundred years ago, one heard the same kinds of comments about the American family that one hears today—in short, that the American family is disintegrating. Proof of this disintegration at the end of the nineteenth century included three points: the declining birth rate, a rising divorce rate, and evidence that women were not completely content with their domestic role. It's a little surprising to me that the same claim about the family is being made today—that it is disintegrating. And often the same points are mentioned as proof: declining birth rates, increasing divorce rates, and discontent of women with domestic roles. Now, in no way do I mean to imply that cultural, demographic, and economic conditions are the same now as they were 100 years ago. On the contrary, the very nature of the family has changed drastically in the last 50 years, not to mention the last 100 years. But I don't think the average person's concept of the family has changed very much over the years. A lot of people have one fixed idea of the family: a married couple where Mother stays home to care for the children and Father works. But this idea is challenged by what we see every day in U.S. society. To be sure, the family is a very sensitive barometer for what is happening in the society, the culture, and the economy of the United States. To make this point clearer, we'll take a look at how the American family has changed in the last 50 years by looking at three different time periods: the mid-1940s to the mid-1960s; the mid-60s to the mid-80s; and finally the present. Sociologist Barbara Dafoe Whitehead labels these three periods the period of traditional familism, the period of individualism, and the period of the new familism. I will try for each period to show how economic, demographic, and cultural elements interact and, in turn, affect the family.

Well, let's proceed in chronological order and start with traditional familism. We're talking here of the twenty years from the mid-1940s to the mid-1960s. This was the period after World War II, a period characterized by a very strong economy. This gave the United States a rising standard of living and a growing middle class. Demographically, the predominant configuration of the family from these years was the traditional one: a married couple with children. Some women worked, but divorce rates were low, and birth rates were high. I guess you could say that the country idealized the family in these years. What I mean is, there was a commitment to the family from its members and a reverence for it from society. TV programs of the era depicted the family in the classical configuration: working father, housewife, and children. Culturally, three characteristics stand out in this period: conformity to social norms, greater male domination of the family than in the later periods, and clear-cut gender roles, that is, clear and separate roles for men and women at home and at work. Well, things changed quite a bit after this period.

Let's move on to the second period, the period of individualism. This period is from the mid-1960s to the mid-1980s. Because individualism is so often mentioned in our discussion of U.S. culture and people, I should make a little detour here before we discuss it. Individualism brings to mind two other words: independence and self-reliance. Individualism conveys the idea that one should think and act for himself or herself, according to what one feels is right. Individualism is easily confused with egotism or selfishness, but in its best sense, it is much more. Individualism implies that one has the freedom to decide what is best rather than allowing that decision to be made by a group such as the community or society. Individualism does, of course, conflict with the concept of community, which implies that the group shares in making decisions. And this conflict between the individual and the community is one that comes up again and again in our lecture series about the United States. Now, let's get back to our discussion about the family.

The second period, the period of individualism, saw three important social and political movements. Do you have any idea which movements I might be talking about? Keep in mind that these decades were characterized by a lack of conformity to social norms. Well, the movements I have in mind are the sexual revolution, in which sex was clearly no longer reserved for marriage; the women's liberation movement; and the movement against the war in Vietnam. All three movements—the sexual revolution, woman's liberation, and the antiwar movement—were typical of the nonconforming nature of these decades. Now, culturally, it is in this period where we see two important developments: one, the idealization of one's career and work and, two, the drive for self-expression and self-fulfillment. In this period, the feminist movement challenged traditional gender roles and male domination of society. Women began to enter professions previously closed to them like medicine, law, and management. Men, for their part, began at least to consider a more active role in raising their children.

These cultural changes occurred during a time of economic changes, too. This was a time of rapidly rising cost of living. Together, these forces changed the demographics of the family. The former picture of the family had only one configuration: a married couple with children where Mother stayed home. The new picture of the family had to include new configurations, like families in which the husband and wife both worked, families of single parents with children, and families of cohabiting couples with or without children. With more women pursuing careers and making money, there was less economic pressure for them to stay in an unsuitable marriage. Therefore, divorce rates doubled in a decade. Rising divorce rates and more financial independence for women made marriage a less attractive arrangement for many women. Consequently, the number of single-parent households tripled. Less conformity to social norms paved the way for cohabitation. So the number of unmarried couples living together in this period quadrupled. Can you see how economic, cultural, and demographic aspects of the society interact with each other? I hope so. Well, let's continue with our agenda.

The third period, the new familism, is harder to see because we are living in this period now. And because we are constantly informed by the media about the deteriorating American family, it's hard to get an objective view of the state of the family. I think that today most people applaud the social changes that came about in the second period of individualism. They are not willing to give up gender equality, the freedom to leave an unsuitable marriage, or the self-fulfillment of an interesting job. At the same time, most experts, if not most people, admit that children paid a high price for the social changes that took place in the second period. It was the children who spent long days in day care or after-school hours home alone while both parents worked. And it was the children who grew up with only one parent or with stepparents in many cases.

Some experts see changes occurring now in U.S. society, changes that affect the family. They see a continuing decline in divorce rates since the 1980s but also a decline in birth rates after an initial increase in the 1980s. The decline in divorce rates could be due to families' better financial situations. Despite the decline in divorce, a quarter of U.S. children today live with only one parent. The birth rate is probably declining because an increasing life span results in fewer women of childbearing age. A more encouraging reason is the reduction in unmarried teen pregnancies. Experts also report an attempt by people to balance work with family obligations, especially the care of children. They see the individualism of the middle period changing somewhat; the concern seems in many cases to be shifting from one's career to one's family, from individualism to the new familism. The most optimistic view of this third period would be that Americans have learned from past mistakes: they want to regain the commitment to family of the first period and keep the equality and fulfillment of the second period. It will not be easy to regain the commitment to the family of the first period. It will require changes in how society and the government look at the family. In families where both parents work, one parent may try to work at home or work only part-time to have more time for the children. Places of work may offer more flexible working hours and on-site day care to allow more time for parents and children. For its part, the government could mandate parental leave, family allowances, and quality day-care centers. Parental leave and family allowances would allow parents to stay home to look after their newborn children. Quality day care would be adequately staffed by professionals who stay at their jobs and with the same children year after year.

None of these changes is guaranteed. But it seems clear that such changes or similar ones are necessary to ensure a healthier U.S. family in the future; and, a healthier family is needed to play the central role that family does in every society. I've gone over a lot here, but if you want to pursue the topic further, there are some references at the end of the lesson to help you do so.

III. POSTLISTENING

A. Accuracy Check

1. Are cultural, economic, and demographic conditions the same now as they were 100 years ago in the United States?

2. What proof of family disintegration is given for both the past and the present?

3. What was the predominant configuration of the family during the first period of traditional familism?

4. In the lecturer's mind, is the meaning of individualism closer to self-reliance or closer to selfishness?

5. What three social and political movements occurred during the second period of individualism?

6. What two cultural changes occurred during this second period?

7. By what number did single-parent families and cohabiting couples increase during the second period?

8. In which of the three periods discussed do parents put themselves before their children?

9. What cultural elements from the first two periods do people want to keep today?

10. In what three ways could the government promote, or help, the new familism?

Chapter 5   Religion

I. PRELISTENING

B. Vocabulary and Key Concepts

1. The U.S. government cannot ask for information on religious affiliation on a <u>mandatory</u> basis.

2. One <u>survey</u> done in 2002 shows that 76 percent of the total population identified themselves as Christian, with 52 percent identifying themselves as <u>Protestant</u> and 24 percent as Catholic.

3. The number of Americans belonging to churches or other religious organizations is surprisingly high compared to other <u>modernized</u> nations.

4. This is not to suggest that religious <u>values</u> are not important in these other nations.

5. Freedom of worship is <u>guaranteed</u> by the First Amendment to the Constitution.

6. The First Amendment also <u>establishes</u> the separation of church and state.

7. The importance of religion in American history should not be <u>underestimated</u>.

8. I'd like to talk about the increasing <u>role</u> religion has <u>played</u> in fairly recent history.

9. Religion had seemed to be in <u>decline</u>, but there was a religious <u>revival</u> in the 1970s that surprised many people.

10. The religious revival was <u>conservative</u> in nature and, at first, largely confined to issues in the private sphere of life.

11. These issues, however, were very <u>controversial</u> in nature and became quite <u>politicized</u> in a short time.

12. Perhaps the "rise of the religious right" is a temporary <u>phenome-</u>

<u>non</u> in American life.

13. Some people predict that American society will become increasingly <u>secular</u> and less religious in the future; others predict a more <u>authoritarian</u> political atmosphere based on conservative religious belief.

D. Notetaking Preparation

1. Commonly Used Symbols and Abbreviations (Narrator: Read twice.)

1. The population of China is greater than the population of India, which in turn is larger than the population in the United States.

2. A decreasing death rate and a rising birth rate cause an increase in the population.

3. The population in the United States is approximately 281,000,000 people.

4. Some people immigrated to the United States because of natural disasters, such as droughts or famines.

5. The situation in the world is different today. Therefore, a greater number of people are immigrating to the United States from Latin America and Asia than Europe.

6. After World War II, most American families were still traditional ones, that is, with a working father, a mother who was a housewife, and their children.

7. Today many children are raised in homes without a father living with them.

II. LISTENING

LECTURE: Religion

Religion is a complex phenomenon in the United States and often misunderstood by foreigners. Part of this may be because the media, for example, television and films, are often the only ways that foreigners are exposed to American culture. These media, in general, ignore the role and importance of religion in America.

Driving through the countryside and passing through small towns in the United States, foreigners are often surprised by the number of churches in even a small town of two or three thousand people. That there are so many churches doesn't seem so strange, perhaps, if we look at the history of the United States. Remember when we talked about immigration to the United States? At that time, we pointed out that many people immigrated to escape persecution and to seek freedom to practice their religion. Considering that people from many different countries and religious backgrounds immigrated to the United States, it shouldn't be surprising to find a great number of different religious denominations. Even in a small town, there will usually be several churches representing different religious groups. Today I'd like to give you some facts and figures about religious groups in the United States, then compare the United States to other modernized nations, and, finally, say something about the importance of religion in America, particularly about the increasing role of religion in U.S. political life in recent years.

Estimating the number of people belonging to various religious groups in America can be a little difficult to do. First of all, the U.S. government cannot ask for information on religious affiliation on a mandatory basis in any official capacity. Statistical information must be gathered from surveys of the population and from organizational reports, which might, for example, include the number of members belonging to a church, synagogue, or mosque. One survey done in 2002 shows that 76 percent of the total population identified themselves as Christian, with 52 percent identifying themselves as Protestant and 24 percent as Catholic. One percent of the population identified themselves as Jewish and another 1 percent as Muslim. I should point out that Protestants, who form the single largest religious group, are found in more than 1,200 denominations.

Another study, called "The American Religious Identification Survey," showed that the number of people identifying themselves as Christian dropped from 86 percent to 77 percent between 1990 and 2001. The total number of those who identified themselves as Jewish declined a little, whereas the total number who identified themselves as Muslims doubled. Other smaller groups such as Buddhists and Hindus also increased their numbers. I don't want to suggest that these are the only religious groups in the United States. There are many more small religious groups. OK, that's enough facts and figures about various religious groups in the United States.

Now let's look at two ways that religion in the United States differs from religion in other modernized nations. The first relates to the number of persons who claim membership in churches or some other religious organization. The second concerns the relationship of religion and government. Let's consider the first way the United States differs from these other modernized nations. About 60 percent of Americans belong to a church or other religious organization. This number is surprisingly high in comparison to other modernized nations. For example, the percentage of people who belong to a church or other religious organization is only about 22 percent in Great Britain, 15 percent in Spain, 7 percent in Italy, and 4 percent in France. This is not to suggest, though, that religious values may not be important in these countries, but it does suggest how important belonging to a church or other religious organization is to Americans compared to

Europeans. However, there is another somewhat contradictory difference that we should also consider. In many of these modernized, European nations, there is no clear separation of religion and government. When discussing religion in America, it's important to remember that whereas freedom of worship is guaranteed by the First Amendment to the Constitution, this same amendment also establishes the separation of church and state. Therefore, although this amendment guarantees everyone the right to practice his or her religion, it also tends to keep religion out of the public sphere, that is, out of anything concerning the government and public schools, for example. Religion has been largely a private matter in the lives of Americans and not been a matter of government, politics, and public education. Of course, religious beliefs and values have always influenced politics and education, but generally indirectly. To sum up, then, the importance of belonging to a church or religious organization seems greater to Americans than to Europeans, but at the same time, religion has no official role in the government as it has in some European countries and has largely been confined to the private side of people's lives. However, there has been a recent trend leading to an increase in the influence of religion in politics. Finally, let's take a closer look at this rather sudden rise in the influence of religion on American political life.

Although religion in America seemed to many people to be in decline during most of this century, in the 1970s, there was a religious revival that surprised many, especially those people in academia, the media, and government. This religious revival became known as the "rise of the religious right." That is, the people involved in this religious revival were politically conservative, or to the right of the center. For a while it seemed that this rise in conservative religion would be largely confined to the private sphere of life. The religious right was generally opposed to abortion, but abortion was made legal by the Supreme Court anyway. The religious right generally favored prayer in schools, but the Supreme Court found that prayer in public schools was unconstitutional. The issues of abortion and prayer were felt by many to be matters of private concern, not serious political issues. However, these issues have become increasingly politicized, and because they are highly controversial issues, they have tended to divide people very sharply. The issue of abortion, especially, has become very politicized and has led to very bitter political debate and even acts of violence. The religious right has also put more and more pressure on politicians to put prayer back in the schools, even if this requires another amendment to the Constitution. This rise of the religious right can no longer be ignored by people in politics. However, whether this group will be able to influence political life for a long time cannot be known. Perhaps this is a temporary phenomenon, and in time the religious right will become less important.

What the role and importance of religion will be in the future of American society cannot be known, of course. There are those who predict that Americans will become more like Europeans if economic prosperity continues, that is, more secular and less religious. Others fear that the rise in conservative religious beliefs may lead to a more authoritarian political atmosphere with less personal freedom for individuals. Because religious values have always been important in America in one way or another, it seems likely that religion will continue to play an important role in America well into the future.

By the way, the history of some religious minorities in the United States is particularly interesting and sheds some light on the tougher issues related to the government's commitment to freedom of religion and the separation of church and state. Some of these better known groups are the Amish, the Mormons, and the Seventh-Day Adventists. I don't have time to go into them today, but for those of you who are interested, I suggest that you do some further investigation of these religious minorities.

III. POSTLISTENING

A. Accuracy Check

1. Why do many foreigners often not understand the role of religion in America?

2. What are the two largest religious groups in America, and what are the percentages of people who identify themselves as belonging to these groups?

3. According to the lecturer, why are there so many different religious groups in the United States?

4. About what percentage of people are members of a church or other religious organization in the following countries: the United States, Italy, and France?

5. What right does the First Amendment to the Constitution guarantee?

6. What does the First Amendment say about religion and the state, that is, religion and government?

7. Was the religious revival of the 1970s conservative or liberal?

8. What was the religious revival called?

9. What issues have become very important politically because of this religious revival?

10. If America becomes more like Europe, will it become more religious or more secular?

I. PRELISTENING

B. Vocabulary and Key Concepts

1. Customs and traditions are often <u>bewildering</u> to foreigners, partly because the customs are so <u>ingrained</u> that people accept them without ever thinking about them.

2. The baby <u>shower</u> is given by a close friend or relative of the <u>expectant</u> mother.

3. The <u>mother-to-be</u> is often invited to someone's home on some <u>pretext</u> so that she can be surprised.

4. Through advice and <u>expressions</u> of <u>envy</u>, the expectant mother is <u>reassured</u> about the desirability of her situation.

5. A few years ago, it was almost <u>unheard</u> of for men to participate in baby showers.

6. In the past, men were <u>banished</u> from the <u>delivery</u> room, but today many men are with their wives to "coach" them through the birth.

7. Christians usually have a religious service, called a <u>baptism</u>, for the new baby.

8. Some customs are generally <u>observed</u> concerning <u>fiancées</u>, the engagement period, and the wedding ceremony.

9. Because priests, rabbis, and ministers are all legally <u>empowered</u> to marry couples, it is not necessary to have both a <u>civil</u> and a religious ceremony.

10. Some customs about the <u>bride</u> and <u>groom</u> are rather <u>superstitious</u> in nature.

11. Some churches and other places where weddings are held have recently <u>banned</u> the throwing of rice as being <u>hazardous</u> to guests, who can slip and fall on it.

12. At the time of death, one decision is whether the funeral will be held in a church or in a funeral home; another decision is whether the body will be <u>cremated</u> or buried in a cemetery.

13. The family may choose to have a <u>memorial</u> service instead of a funeral. In either case, the family may hold a <u>wake</u>, where the body of the deceased is displayed in its casket.

14. At a funeral, a <u>eulogy</u> is usually given by someone close to the <u>deceased</u> person.

15. Those who want to express their <u>condolences</u> usually send a sympathy card to the <u>bereaved</u> family.

D. Notetaking Preparation

1. Key Words: Listening
(Narrator: Read twice.)

a. Many ethnic groups still practice customs and traditions that their ancestors brought with them from their countries, yet if we look at the United States and the people as a whole, we can find a kind of general culture. (repeat)

b. One of the most common traditions associated with a birth is the baby shower, a nonreligious tradition observed by almost everyone in this society. (repeat)

c. As for the actual wedding ceremony and related celebrations, traditionally it is the bride's family who pays for these expenses. (repeat)

d. For most people, whether they are religious or not, there are many decisions to be made at the time of a death. (repeat)

e. At a funeral service, it is customary for a religious leader to speak some words of comfort for the bereaved. In addition, a eulogy is usually given by someone close to the deceased person. (repeat)

II. LISTENING

LECTURE: Passages: Birth, Marriage, and Death

Customs vary so much from country to country or culture that it's often bewildering for a foreigner trying to understand the traditions and customs of a new country. Part of what makes it so difficult is that most of these customs are so ingrained in the culture that most local people accept them without ever thinking about them. Some of the reasons for the customs or traditions are historical and may have even been forgotten by the people who still practice these customs. When pressed for an explanation of some of their customs, people will sometimes be quite surprised that anyone would question their customs. "Doesn't everyone do it this way?" might be their response, yet some of the customs that seem so natural to the people in the country or culture may seem quite strange and inexplicable to people new to a country. In a country as large as the United States, with people from so many different parts of the world and different cultures, it can be even more bewildering. Many ethnic groups still practice customs and traditions brought by their ancestors from their countries, yet if we look at the country and its people as a whole, we can find a kind of "general" culture with traditions that are often accepted or at least adapted to fit the customs and traditions of each immigrant group as it becomes assimilated into the larger culture. Today let's look at some widely accepted customs and traditions of most Americans concerning three of life's most important events: birth, marriage, and death. Please keep in mind that these descriptions are very general and that society is changing quite rapidly in the United States and that people adapt and modify these customs to fit changing societal conditions and their own situations.

The birth of a baby is a momentous occasion in any family and is celebrated in some way or another. There are many traditions associated with this event. One of the most common ones is the baby shower, which is a nonreligious tradition observed by almost everyone in this society. A shower is given by a close friend or relative of the expectant mother shortly before the baby is due. In the past, showers were almost always arranged in secret so as to be a complete surprise to the mother-to-be. The mother-to-be was usually invited to someone's home on one pretext or another, where she was surprised by her female friends and relatives who had planned this special party for her. In recent years, the tradition has been modified, at least in some social circles, so that the shower is not always a surprise occasion, but one that the expectant mother knows about ahead of time.

Whether the baby shower is a surprise or not, the mother-to-be is showered with gifts for the new baby by her friends and relatives. The gifts may be small ones or very expensive ones depending on the financial situation of the participants, but there is always a very emotional outpouring of good wishes for the expected baby and its parents. The gifts are always opened at the party, and everyone expresses great admiration for them. There's always a lot of advice from experienced mothers and expressions of envy from those women who do not yet have children. This way, the expectant mother is reassured about the coming event and the desirability of her situation. A few years ago, it was almost unheard of for men to participate in baby showers. However, as I mentioned earlier, society is changing rapidly and men's participation at baby showers is becoming more common. That reminds me of another related change in society in the United States. In the past, when births mainly took place at home, it was a strictly female event with men banished from the room where the baby was born. After women started going to hospitals to have their babies, men still never went into the delivery room and were expected to wait nervously in the waiting room for the doctor to come and tell them the good news. Today this is changing for many modern couples. Often they attend classes together to prepare them for the birth of the baby, and many men are with their wives in the delivery room and "coach" them through the birth along with the doctors.

After a baby is born, many, if not most, people want to have a religious service for their baby within a few weeks of the baby's birth, even if they are not very religious themselves. Friends and family will attend the service, which will be held in a church or a synagogue. For Christians, this service is ordinarily called baptism.

There are many customs and traditions surrounding marriage and particularly the wedding activities themselves. Once again, it is very hard to generalize about these customs, as they vary so much among different people, but there are some customs that are quite generally observed. It is no longer necessary for a young man to ask permission of a girl's father for her "hand," and among modern couples a woman may actually be the first one to bring up the subject of marriage, but most young people still very much want their parents' approval of the person they hope to marry. It is still traditional for a young man to give his fiancée a diamond ring at the beginning of their engagement period. As for the actual wedding ceremony and related celebrations, traditionally it is the bride's family who pays for these expenses. The wedding ceremony can be a very simple one, with only a few family members and close friends present, or it can be very elaborate, with hundreds of people in attendance. The traditional reception that follows the ceremony can be as simple as cookies and punch in the church or as elaborate as a large sit-down dinner held at a local hotel with a dance and a private orchestra following the dinner. Sometimes people are invited only to the wedding or only to the reception. At any rate, these events can usually be attended only by invitation. One very popular tradition associated with weddings is, once again, the shower that we mentioned in relation to birth. At this shower given before the wedding, the bride-to-be receives gifts to help her set up her new household, such as electrical appliances, sheets, towels, and pots and pans. In addition to shower gifts, wedding gifts are also expected from people who receive wedding invitations. Occasionally people choose not to have any kind of religious service at their wedding and opt to get married in a civil ceremony in a government building. However, a civil ceremony is not necessary if a couple decides to get married in a religious ceremony. Priests, ministers, and rabbis are legally empowered to marry couples, and it is not necessary to have both a civil and a religious ceremony. By the way, there's an interesting tradition associated with weddings that is rather hard to explain, but then many traditions are. It is said every bride at her wedding should be wearing or carrying "something old, something new, something borrowed, something blue." The bride will be checked at the last minute to be sure that she has one of each of these. There are some other customs similar to this one that are rather superstitious in nature. For example, people believe that it is bad luck for the groom to see the bride in her wedding dress before the ceremony. And immediately following the ceremony, as the couple leave the church, people at the ceremony will throw rice at them to signal fertility—that is, a hope that they will have many children. Some churches and other places where weddings are held have recently banned the throwing of rice as being hazardous to guests who can slip and fall on it. Some suggest throwing rose petals or some other substitute for the rice.

In addition to birth and marriage, every society has to deal with death. Once again, it is hard to generalize about the customs surrounding death. Each religious group has ways to help its members cope with the loss of a family member or friend. For most people, religious or not, there are many decisions to be made at the time of a death. One decision is whether to have a funeral held in a church or in a funeral home. Another decision is whether to have the body cremated or not. If the body is cremated, a memorial service is held rather than a funeral. If the body is not cremated, a decision must be made about whether to display the body or not at the funeral. A day or two before the funeral, it is also quite common to hold a wake at a funeral home where the body is displayed in its casket. At the wake the family receives those people who wish to express their sympathy to the bereaved.

At the funeral service it is customary for a religious leader to speak some words of comfort for the bereaved. In addition, a eulogy is usually given by someone close to the deceased person. Sometimes many people will speak about the good deeds of the person who has died. After the religious ceremony, the body is usually taken to a cemetery, where it will be buried after another brief religious service. Of course, most people learn of the death of someone they know from the person's family, but notices of funeral services are also printed in the newspaper, and anyone who wishes to attend the service is expected to without a personal invitation from the family. People who knew the deceased casually, but who want to express their condolences, usually send a "sympathy" card to the family. It is traditional to send flowers to a funeral, but it is important to check with a florist to be sure to send the correct kind of flowers. It's sometimes important to know what kind of clothes to wear to a wedding or a funeral. Traditionally the bride wears white, and guests at the wedding are free to wear whatever colors they like, except for women, who do not wear white. At a funeral, it used to be necessary to wear black to show grief, but today this custom is no longer observed.

As I said before, in a society so large and diverse as the United States, customs can vary greatly from area to area, among different social, ethnic, and economic groups, and even from generation to generation. I have tried to give you some idea of customs and traditions that are generally accepted, but, of course, it's always wise to ask if you find yourself in a situation where you might be invited or expected to participate in one of these events. When in doubt, ask.

III. POSTLISTENING ACTIVITY

A. Accuracy Check

1. When are baby showers usually given?

2. What are two recent changes concerning the custom of baby showers?

3. What do we call the Christian religious service held after a baby is born?

4. Who traditionally pays for an American wedding?

5. Do most American couples have a civil ceremony or a religious ceremony when they get married?

6. What four things does tradition say a bride should have at her wedding?

7. By custom, who should not see the bride in her wedding dress before the wedding ceremony?

8. Under what circumstances is a memorial service held instead of a funeral?

9. What two things are often sent to the family of the deceased or to a funeral?

10. What color shouldn't a woman wear as a guest at a wedding?

Unit Three | American Trademarks

Chapter 7   Multiculturalism

I. PRELISTENING

B. Vocabulary and Key Concepts

1. I understand why a foreigner might react <u>skeptically</u> to U.S. culture, especially if the person comes from a more ethnically and racially <u>homogeneous</u> society.

2. It seems naive or even perverse to <u>deny</u> the existence of a culture that has such great <u>impact</u> on other cultures, for better or worse.

3. A <u>melting</u> pot, literally a pot in which metals like aluminum and copper are melted in order to blend them, is the traditional <u>metaphor</u> for the way the different groups of immigrants came together in the United States.

4. Some people feel that the monoculturalist view of many nationalities blending together into an <u>alloy</u> of all the parts in it is a <u>myth</u>.

5. Opponents point out that many groups have at times been <u>excluded</u> from participating in U.S. society through segregation and <u>discrimination</u>.

6. U.S. society probably did not assimilate new cultural input until the new immigrants were <u>viewed</u> with less <u>prejudice</u>.

7. The metaphor the multiculturalists use is the patchwork quilt, a <u>mosaic</u> of separate, <u>autonomous</u> subcultures.

8. <u>Intermarriage</u> and the <u>adoption</u> of children of another race make a difference in how people in a family look at themselves.

9. The point here is that the ethnically and racially pure individuals <u>implied</u> by the multiculturalist view are more the <u>exception</u> than the rule.

10. We <u>inherit</u> some of our culture from our families and <u>absorb</u> some of our culture unconsciously.

11. If <u>assimilation</u> does not take place in the first <u>generation</u>, it most certainly does by the second or third.

12. Monoculturalists fear a <u>fragmentation</u>, or even destruction, of U.S. culture, whereas <u>proponents</u> of the pluralistic view disagree.

13. It would be wrong to assume that the <u>dominant</u> culture we've been speaking about <u>reflects</u> the culture of only one group.

14. <u>Opponents</u> of the pluralistic view of culture cite <u>Latinos</u>, especially Mexican immigrants, the single largest immigrant group since the 1990s.

II. LISTENING

LECTURE: Multiculturalism

Foreigners from older cultures with traditions dating back hundreds and hundreds of years sometimes react with surprise and skepticism when the topic of U.S. culture comes up. Commenting on the United States, they sometimes say things like "But the United States has no culture." People in the United States find comments such as this one amusing at best, and sometimes downright infuriating. In a way, I understand why a foreigner might react skeptically to the United States, especially if the person comes from a more ethnically and racially homogeneous society. Or if the person comes from a society whose culture is reinforced by state institutions—government, church, and schools, for instance. It would be hard for this foreigner to understand a multiracial, ethnically diverse country like the United States, whose institutions do not strongly reinforce the culture. However, it seems naive or even perverse to deny the existence of a culture that has such great impact on other cultures, for better or worse. The clothes that Americans wear, the food they eat, the music, films, and books they produce, and even to some extent the religions they practice influence how many people in other countries live and think. One may easily disapprove of the influence that mass American culture has on the world, but one cannot objectively deny that influence.

In all fairness, I have to say that it's understandable that foreigners have trouble identifying an American culture because not even the best minds in the country—writers, educators, and politicians—agree on the basic nature of U.S. culture. Today I'll try to contrast three ways that U.S. culture has been perceived over the years. Then perhaps you can decide which point of view seems the most logical to you. We'll take a look at the older monoculturalist view; a newer, multiculturalist view; and finally a third view, which I'll call the pluralistic view.

First in our discussion is the monoculturalist view of the United States as a melting pot. A melting pot, literally a pot in which metals like aluminum and copper are melted in order to blend them, is the traditional metaphor for the way the different groups of immigrants came together in the United States. Now, theoretically, the result of many nationalities blending together is one big unified common culture, an alloy of all the parts in it. In other words, the result is a combination of all the different parts, which have mixed together and are no longer recognizable as separate parts. However, many people today feel that the idea of one common U.S. culture is a myth and has always been a myth. To support their view, opponents point out that many groups, notably African, Asian, and Native Americans, have at times been excluded from participating fully in society through segregation and discrimination. Furthermore, a trademark of U.S. immigration has been that the most recently arrived group, whether Irish or Italian or Chinese or Jewish, typically faced strong discrimination from those already in the United States. We know that all these groups have made important contributions to the culture, that is not the point. The point is, given the climate of discrimination at different times in the past (and even now), U.S. society does not assimilate new cultural input until much later—after the new immigrants are viewed with less prejudice. Let's move on to another view of U.S. culture.

The second view of U.S. culture that we'll look at today is the multiculturalist view. The multiculturalist view focuses on the many subcultures that make up the U.S. population—all the different ethnic and racial groups we talked about in a previous lecture. Now, each group brought its own distinct culture when it immigrated to the United States. The multiculturalist view does not see U.S. culture as a melting pot; rather, the metaphor that multiculturalists often employ is the patchwork quilt, a bedcover made of numerous pieces of differently-colored material. (Have you seen quilts like these on beds?) The metaphor of the patchwork quilt is appropriate in that the multiculturalists see the United States as a mosaic of separate, autonomous subcultures, each one distinct from the other. U.S. culture, in this view, is a sum of the distinct parts, with little or no mixing of subcultures. Opponents of this view, those who disagree with it (and there are many who do), say that the multiculturalist view ignores the characteristic mixing of groups, both ethnic and racial, that has been common in the United States. Americans of European background have always intermarried. Many people are a combination of four or more ethnic backgrounds—and often of more backgrounds than they can keep track of. I do not want to imply that the United States has overcome its race problems—far from it. But recent census statistics give two indications of somewhat more mixing than previously. First, one in fifteen U.S. marriages is now interracial. An interracial marriage would be any combination of white, black, Asian, and Native American spouses. Admittedly, there are many more marriages between Asians or Native Americans and whites than between blacks and whites. Second, of the 1.6 million children who are adopted, 17 percent make their families multiracial because of the adoption of local children of another race or of children from abroad, especially from Asia or Latin America. Intermarriage and adoption of children of another race make a difference in how people in a family look at themselves. The point here is, the ethnically and racially pure individuals implied by the multiculturalist view are more the exception than the rule. Take, for instance, an African American man married to a Filipina, whose two sons married white women. Where in the patchwork quilt do the grandchildren of the African American former Supreme Court Justice Thurgood Marshall belong? This is an extreme example, but I think it shows that Marshall's grandchildren share many subcultures; they do not represent just one square on the quilt. For this reason, many people prefer another, more satisfactory, view of U.S. culture.

The last cultural view we'll discuss today, the pluralistic view, is a combination of the first two views. The pluralistic view says that individuals have a number of cultural influences, some of which they share with others and some of which are different from one person to another. These cultural influences have three distinct sources: we inherit some of our culture from our families; we absorb some of our culture unconsciously from living in the culture (television figures importantly in this unconscious absorption); and third, we choose some cultural influences that we find attractive from the many subcultures in the United States. In this way, the population shares a large portion of common culture, but people also have individual cultural characteristics that make them different from others. The pluralistic view of culture recognizes the strong role of assimilation, becoming part of the larger group. In assimilation, one becomes part of a larger, dominant culture by accepting much, if not all, of the culture. The pluralistic view differs from the monocultural view in that pluralistic assimilation does not mean that immigrants must deny their original cultures or that they must forget them. But in all likelihood, immigrants become a little less Mexican, Chinese, or Arab as they assimilate parts of the new culture. Assimilation is not required by the dominant culture, but we do know that it occurs regularly among immigrant groups. If assimilation does not take place in the first generation, it most certainly does by the second or third generation.

Opponents of the pluralistic view of culture cite Latinos especially Mexican immigrants, the single largest immigrant group since the 1990s. These opponents say that instead of assimilating as other groups have, Mexicans maintain strong ties to neighboring Mexico through frequent visits home. As a result, opponents fear a fragmentation, or even destruction, of U.S. culture as we know it. On the other hand, proponents of the pluralistic view point out that even Latinos follow the pattern of previous immigrants; indeed, a fifth of Latinos in the United States intermarry. If this seems like a small number, I think we could safely predict higher intermarriage rates in future generations.

It would be wrong to assume that the dominant, or common, culture we've been speaking about reflects the culture of only one ethnic or racial group that makes up the United States. At the same time, if U.S. society is an open one, as Americans like to believe, it would be hard to deny the changing nature of U.S. culture. It has always reflected the cultures of its immigrants and will likely continue to do so. If we accept this premise, the continuation and possible increase in Latino immigration will change the character of the U.S. culture somewhat. Not as drastically as monoculturalists fear, I think, but a change no doubt will occur. I suspect U.S. culture, to use another metaphor, will continue to seem like the same dish—but it will be a dish with a somewhat Latino flavor in the future. The real test of the future of the United States as a culture may well be whether its cultural ideal of tolerance is a reality. Well, I really have taken much more of your time than I should have. Good-bye for now.

III. POSTLISTENING

A. Accuracy Check

1. Is the United States an ethnically and racially homogeneous society?

2. Does the lecturer think U.S. culture is easier or harder to understand than the cultures of some other countries?

3. Which of the three views of culture is the oldest one?

4. In the first subtopic, which groups suffered from discrimination?

5. What metaphor for the culture do the multiculturalists use?

6. Does the multiculturalist view support the idea of one common U.S. culture?

7. Of the 1.6 million adopted children, what percentage make their families multiracial?

8. In what three ways do we get our culture, according to the pluralistic view?

9. What do some people fear will result if the large Hispanic immigration continues in the future?

10. Does the lecturer see the United States as a culture that is open to change or one that is closed to change?

I. PRELISTENING

B. Vocabulary and Key Concepts

1. Between 1994 and 2001, <u>violent</u> crime—homicide, rape, arson, and <u>aggravated</u> assault—fell 52 percent.

2. At the same time, in recent years there has been stricter law <u>enforcement</u> in cities like New York and Boston, and very <u>stringent</u> penalties have been imposed on repeat offenders.

3. Statistics are harder to come by for <u>white-collar</u> crime, crimes including <u>embezzlement</u> and bribery.

4. One theory says that people are basically <u>aggressive</u> by nature and, therefore, <u>predisposed to</u> violence.

5. If a person commits a crime, society is <u>to blame</u> because society's <u>shortcomings</u> are the cause of the criminal behavior.

6. There are <u>root</u> causes like racism and more obvious causes like the breakdown of the family and a <u>proliferation</u> of drugs.

7. Because they have been <u>deprived of</u> the benefits that most Americans have, criminals are alienated from society, which causes them to <u>strike out</u> at the society.

8. The <u>underclass</u> is that small part of the population that typically fits the following profile: poor, unemployed, badly educated, <u>disproportionately</u> black, inner-city youth, some of whom belong to gangs.

9. According to the theory, society <u>curbs</u> this aggressiveness and potential violence by <u>socializing</u> us.

10. Society gives us <u>values</u> against killing and stealing, for example, and values for honesty and <u>compassion.</u>

11. If we are adequately socialized, we have a <u>conscience</u>, the result of values that determine how we <u>bring up</u> our children.

12. The amount of crime depends on how <u>punishment</u> is used as a <u>deterrent</u> to crime—that is, how effectively the criminal justice system functions.

13. Typically, white-collar criminals, who include some businessmen and <u>financiers</u>, may be <u>lacking</u> a well-developed conscience.

14. Without a strong conscience, a person's innate aggressiveness <u>takes over</u> and <u>leads to</u> crime.

15. Many experts feel that this can come about only if the underclass has the same <u>benefits</u> that the majority of the population <u>take for granted</u>.

LECTURE: Crime and Violence in the United States

According to a Gallup poll in 2001, Americans, for the first time in twelve years, believed that there was less violent crime that year than the year before. To be sure, many said that there were areas near their homes where they were still afraid to walk at night. And a number of people worried about having their car stolen or their home burglarized. So far, we are only talking about people's perceptions about crime—what they believe to be the case. How closely do people's perceptions match reality? Well, let's look at some statistics. When we compare crime statistics between 1994 and 2001, we see that violent crime decreased in the United States. Between 1994 and 2001, violent crime—homicide, rape, arson, and aggravated assault—fell 52 percent. In 1994, there were 51 victims of violent crime per 1,000 people over the age of twelve. In 2001, that number dropped by over half, to 24 per 1,000. Some experts attribute this drop in crime to demographics: the U.S. population is getting older, and older people commit fewer crimes than younger people. At the same time, in recent years there has been stricter law enforcement in cities like New York and Boston, and very stringent penalties have been imposed on repeat offenders in general. But, I don't want to get off the topic here. The fact remains that crime is still an issue in people's lives. And the encouraging statistics about violent crime may not hold true for white-collar crime, crimes that include embezzlement, bribery, political corruption, and corporate policies that endanger workers and the public. Statistics on white-collar crime are hard to come by, and it doesn't put fear in people's hearts the way violent crime does. But it certainly needs to be included in a discussion of crime in the United States.

Crime is such a difficult issue to discuss because it can be looked at in so many different ways. Today I'd like to take a philosophical, sociological look at society and crime. There are two theories of crime that are based on one's feelings about the nature of human beings. The first theory says that people are good by nature. If a person turns to crime, the cause lies outside the person, not inside. In other words, crime and violence come from the environment, or society. The second theory says that people are basically aggressive by nature, and therefore, predisposed to violence. The theory doesn't say that we are violent; rather, it says that we are aggressive and can be violent. Before we go on, I want you to decide in your own minds which of the two theories, if either, you agree with. One, are people basically good by nature? Or, two, are people aggressive and predisposed to violence by nature? Or do you think the nature of people lies somewhere in between the two theories? Have you made up your minds yet? Well, let's go on and take a closer look at both theories. We'll finish with a discussion of possible solutions to the high level of crime in the United States.

To start off with, liberals—in politics, sociology, and other fields—typically embrace the first theory: that people are good by nature. It follows, then, that if someone commits a crime or behaves violently, it is because that person's environment has put violence or evil into his or her heart. If a person commits a crime, society is to blame because society's shortcomings are the cause of the criminal behavior. In the United States, we don't have to look very far to find shortcomings that are seen by many as causes of crime. There are root causes like racism, poverty, and injustice. And there are more obvious causes like the breakdown of the nuclear family, violence on TV, inferior education for some children, unemployment, child abuse, and a proliferation of drugs. In this liberal theory, criminals are alienated from society because they have been deprived of the benefits that most Americans have. Their alienation leads them to strike out at the society that has, in a sense, forgotten them.

The existence of an underclass in U.S. society lends support to this liberal theory of crime. The underclass is that small part of the population that typically fits the following profile: poor, unemployed, badly educated, disproportionately black, inner-city youth. Both gangs and drugs are prevalent in the underclass. Liberals are quick to point out that the shortcomings of life in the underclass help explain how 70 percent of all U.S. crimes are committed by just 6 percent of criminals. Like any theory, this one has critics who disagree with it. The critics point out that most people who grow up as part of the underclass—that is, those in poor, inner-city settings—do not become criminals. Moreover, there are people from rich families, with all the benefits of society, who do become violent criminals. So we need to look a little further into the causes of crime; let's look at the second theory.

The second theory, often embraced by conservatives, sees people as innately aggressive and predisposed to violence. According to this theory, society curbs this aggressiveness and potential violence in two ways: by socializing us and, if that fails, by punishing us. Society socializes us by giving us values. Values against killing and stealing, values against inequality and injustice, for example. And society gives us positive values for honesty, compassion, and kindness. Now, this is important: it is largely the family that socializes us, acting for society. And the result of socialization is a conscience, a sense of right and wrong. Our conscience functions as a curb on violence and criminal behavior because we have been taught right from wrong. If socialization fails, the fear of punishment should act to curb crime, according to the theory. In this conservative view, a criminal is someone who is not adequately socialized or one who isn't afraid of the punishment he or she might receive for a crime. Because of the family's role in socialization, the amount of crime and violence depends greatly on how we bring up our children—that is, how well we pass on important values. It also depends on how punishment is used as a deterrent to crime— that is, how effectively the criminal justice system functions.

This second theory helps us understand white-collar crime, I think, because those who commit white-collar crime are not part of the underclass. Typically, white-collar criminals are businessmen, politicians, and financiers. Unlike the underclass, white-collar criminals have enjoyed the benefits of society. What may be lacking, however, is a well-developed conscience. Without a strong conscience, a person's innate aggressiveness takes over and leads to crime, at least according to the theory. Critics of this theory, however, point out that there are children from families with apparently sound values who still become white-collar criminals. They may become criminals because they feel they won't get caught, so obviously they do not fear punishment.

I think you can see that an issue like crime is far too complex to explain with a simple theory, or even two theories. It's likely and logical that both the family and society can play a part in reducing crime. But I think the theories help in identifying solutions to the problem of crime in the United States.

As for solutions, I think most of us would agree that the family can play a role in reducing crime in the United States: through socialization, which leads children to respect themselves, others, and the values of their society. Moreover, I think society, in the form of government, has a role to play in reducing crime: by overcoming the alienation of the underclass, by helping these people to feel that they are part of the society instead of its victims. Many experts feel that ending the alienation of the underclass can come about only if the underclass has the same benefits that the majority of the population take for granted: good education, health care, and employment. The government, in the form of the justice system, can also contribute to curbing crime by instilling the fear of punishment in those who might become criminals. In another chapter, we look at the justice system, but we don't have any more time today.

III. POSTLISTENING

A. Accuracy Check

1. By what percentage did violent crime decrease between 1994 and 2001?

2. Give three examples of white-collar crime.

3. What three shortcomings of society are seen by some as root causes of crime?

4. Do most people who grow up poor, unemployed, and badly educated become criminals?

5. Is the underclass part of the liberal or conservative theory of crime?

6. How does society socialize its members?

7. In the second, conservative, theory of crime, what two things are supposed to curb crime?

8. How do white-collar criminals differ from criminals of the under-class?

9. What three things do some experts think society should provide for the underclass?

10. Is curbing crime through fear of punishment a liberal solution or a conservative solution?

Chapter 9   Globalization

I. PRELISTENING

B. Vocabulary and Key Concepts

1. The King of Bhutan said that he wasn't sure his country had one of those but was interested in knowing what a <u>gross</u> <u>national</u> <u>product</u> was.

2. Globalization is the <u>acceleration</u> and <u>intensification</u> of economic interaction among the people, companies, and governments of different nations.

3. But it is at the same time a subject that <u>ignites</u> the anger and mistrust of many people in the world: environmentalists, unionists, anarchists, and some governments—all <u>skeptics</u> rather than supporters of globalization.

4. Some skeptics feel that globalization allows rich countries to take <u>advantage</u> of poor countries, which skeptics feel are only hurt by trying to be more <u>capitalistic</u>.

5. And globalization is definitely about capitalism: its goal is to increase the <u>flow</u> <u>of</u> <u>goods</u> and capital around the world.

6. If globalization is included in a book that focuses on the United States, it is because the world sees the United States (and, to a lesser degree, Western Europe and Japan) as the <u>driving</u> <u>force</u> behind the process of globalization.

7. Often, poor countries are pressured to follow global trade rules as a condition for a loan or for aid. For example, a poor country might be advised to adjust the value of its <u>currency</u>, or it might be advised to eliminate <u>tariffs</u>, or taxes, on goods imported from other countries.

8. <u>Patents</u> on new inventions and copyright laws most often protect technology from the West—and keep the technology from being used more freely by poor countries. Poor countries may also be told to <u>privatize</u> their industries and banks.

9. To get an idea how these rules can in some cases <u>hamper</u> development instead of encouraging it, let's take a look at some countries that are not big Western powers but have <u>integrated</u> into the world economy—by *not* following the rules.

10. It is common for critics to claim that globalization has only <u>benefited</u> rich Western countries, but this claim is <u>oversimplified</u>.

11. Harvard economist Dani Rodrik, in "Trading in Illusions," writes that all four countries have taken advantage of opportunities to <u>engage</u> in world trade, that is, to <u>achieve</u> integration in the world economy.

12. India was, and still is, one of the most <u>protectionist</u> economies in the world but has made great progress economically, and South Korea and Taiwan had patent and copyright <u>infringements</u> and restrictions on foreign <u>investment</u>—but still prospered.

13. The poor countries <u>spoke out</u> against agricultural <u>subsidies</u> by rich countries, which make the poor countries' products less competitive in the world market.

14. The twenty-three countries did not manage to <u>abolish</u> the subsidies at that meeting because the talks broke down, but they did <u>speak up</u> for themselves.

D. Notetaking Preparation

1. Structuring
(Narrator: Read twice.)

Critics of globalization will point out that poor countries are often given bad advice by international organizations like the IMF and the World Bank, or that these organizations try to impose unrealistic global trade rules. Often, poor countries are pressured to follow the rules as a condition for a loan or for aid. For example, a poor country might be advised to adjust the value of its currency. Or it might be advised to eliminate tariffs, or taxes, on goods imported from other countries. Many poor countries are also pressured to respect patents and copyright laws. Patents on new inventions and copyright laws most often protect technology from the West—and keep the technology from being used more freely by poor countries. Poorer countries may also be told to privatize industries and banks. Privatization means that the government sells the industries and banks to private companies. Furthermore, the countries are often encouraged *not* to subsidize goods that they produce for export to earn money. These are some examples, but not all of the trade rules imposed by organizations—but I think you get the picture.

LECTURE: Globalization

Let me begin this lecture by telling you a story to put things in perspective. It is a story that the people of Bhutan, a principality partly controlled by India, tell about themselves. When this remote mountain country first made contact with the outside world forty years ago, the United Nations (or UN) asked about their gross national product. The King of Bhutan said that he wasn't sure his country had one of those but was interested in knowing what a gross national product was. Once the UN explained that a gross national product was the total value of all the goods produced and all the services provided in a country in one year, the king said that he thought Bhutan would rather not have one. They would rather have a gross national happiness!

Here was a country where people seemed perfectly happy to have little contact with the outside world. How odd Bhutan of forty years ago seems to us today, when modern telecommunications and world trade have connected virtually every corner of the world to every other part of the world.

Unlike Bhutan forty years ago, today's world is characterized by globalization. Thousands of books have been written about globalization, and there may be as many definitions of the term, all depending on the perspective of the writer. For our purposes let's use this definition: Globalization is the acceleration and intensification of economic interaction among the people, companies, and governments of different nations. Did you get that definition down? Let me repeat it: Globalization is the acceleration and intensification of economic interaction among the people, companies, and governments of different nations. (pause) So, how does globalization work in concrete terms? Let me give you some examples. Cheaper modern communications have made it possible for a call center in India to provide technical support to a person who is having a computer problem in Australia or the United States—or anywhere else in the world. Or a transnational sportswear corporation like Nike can design its products in Europe, produce them in Asia, and sell them in North America. And there are many U.S. and other international companies that have built factories in Mexico to manufacture products that used to be made in the former countries. Globalization sounds like a very positive concept, a wonderful example of international cooperation that benefits all concerned. But it is at the same time a subject that ignites the anger and mistrust of many people in the world: environmentalists, unionists, anarchists, and some governments, among others. You can see that the skeptics come from many different fields. Some skeptics feel that globalization allows rich countries to take advantage of poor countries, which skeptics feel are only hurt by trying to be more capitalistic. And globalization is definitely about capitalism: its goal is to increase the flow of goods and capital around the world. We might call it the "brother" of capitalism.

If globalization is included in a book that focuses on the United States, it is because the world sees the United States (and, to a lesser degree, Western Europe and Japan) as the driving force behind the process of globalization. When one thinks of capitalism and large transnational corporations, the United States is probably the first country that comes to many people's minds. And two big international organizations that deal with development, the International Monetary Fund (or IMF) and the World Bank, are closely associated with the United States in many people's minds. Furthermore, popular American culture, from Coca-Cola and McDonalds to popular music and TV programs, is so widespread in the world that critics of globalization are quick to point to the spread of this culture as U.S. cultural imperialism. We can't really go into cultural imperialism today, but we can look at three different aspects of globalization to understand this complicated process a little better. First, we'll talk about what critics object to in globalization. Then I want to discuss some cases where globalization has been a success, and I don't mean rich Western countries. I'll finish up by talking about some concrete objections critics of globalization have in order to see if there is any solution.

Critics of globalization will point out that poor countries are often given bad advice by international organizations like the IMF and the World Bank, or that these organizations try to impose unrealistic global trade rules. Often, poor countries are pressured to follow the rules as a condition for a loan or for aid. For example, a poor country might be advised to adjust the value of its currency. Or it might be advised to eliminate tariffs, or taxes, on goods imported from other countries. Many poor countries are also pressured to respect patents and copyright laws. Patents on new inventions and copyright laws most often protect technology from the West—and keep the technology from being used more freely by poor countries. Poorer countries may also be told to privatize industries and banks. Privatization means that the government sells the industries and banks to private companies. Furthermore, poorer countries are often encouraged *not* to subsidize goods that they produce. A subsidy is money paid by a government to reduce the costs of producing goods so that their prices can be kept low and therefore competitive in the world market. These are some examples, but not all of the trade rules imposed by organizations—but I think you get the picture. Did you get all five examples down? One: adjust currency. Two: eliminate tariffs. Three: respect patents and copyright law. Four: privatize industry and banks. And five: *not* subsidize the goods they produce. We don't have to go too far to find countries—Argentina comes to mind—that have tried to follow all these rules only to find that their economies have suffered instead of prospering. Critics of globalization will say that the international organizations do not have good intentions—that they want conditions where rich countries or companies can take advantage of poor countries' cheap labor. A more objective and perhaps fairer conclusion might be that these bodies are trying to lead the poor countries to success by copying conditions in richer democracies, where these rules are more or less observed now. That is not to say, however, that Japan, Germany, and the United States developed their economies following the rules, only that the rules are more or less observed now. I say more or less because the United States and Europe have had subsidies on agricultural products for a long time. Another reason for trying to impose trade rules is that the organizations feel that investments from rich countries will not come to poorer countries that do not follow the trade rules, and there is probably a lot of truth in that. Whose opinion you agree with—that of critics of globalization or supporters of it—will depend perhaps on where you are from and how you view capitalism itself. To get an idea how these rules can in some cases hamper development instead of encouraging it, let's take a look at some countries that are not big Western powers but have integrated into the world economy—by *not* following the rules. It may help you understand the whole situation better.

It is common for critics to claim that globalization has only benefited rich Western countries, but this claim is oversimplified. Millions of workers in Japan, Germany, and the United States have seen their jobs move overseas where labor is cheaper, so they certainly wouldn't feel they were benefiting more from globalization than workers in China or Vietnam. To get on with my second point today, let's look more closely at some non-Western countries that have achieved long-term economic growth in the past decades. I am thinking here especially of China, India, Taiwan, and South Korea. Harvard economist Dani Rodrik, in "Trading in Illusions," writes that all four countries have taken advantage of opportunities to engage in world trade, that is, to achieve integration in the world economy. And all four countries have achieved remarkable economic growth in recent decades. We must emphasize, though, that these four countries have accomplished economic growth without following all the tough rules imposed by international organizations. China, for example, broke practically all the rules, including not respecting the requirement of private-property rights, but is making impressive economic progress. India was, and still is, one of the most protectionist economies in the world but has made great progress economically. South Korea and Taiwan, when there were few global trade rules, had high tariffs on imported goods, public (*not* private) ownership of a lot of their industry and banking, government subsidies on goods they exported, patent and copyright infringements, and restrictions on foreign investment. The point is that all four countries have achieved integration in the world economy on their own terms. They did not, and could not realistically, follow another country's example because local conditions vary from one country to another. As Dani Rodrik has written, "There is simply no substitute for a homegrown business plan."

To finish up by talking about our third point today, we have to take up two problems that critics of globalization bring up all the time: sweatshops, where people work long hours in crowded conditions for a relatively low wage; and, second, child labor. The critics are right: we should all be upset by sweatshops. At the same time, we must consider that these same workers compete with each other for the jobs provided by large transnational corporations, which generally pay better than local employers. In other words, the workers prefer this work to the alternative. As for child labor, all of us should be bothered by young children working in many countries. Conceivably, we could manage to prohibit child labor worldwide. However, if we don't make sure that there are schools and the children in question go to them, we may be condemning the children to a fate worse than child labor. A recent article in the *Economist* pointed out that it is poverty rather than globalization that creates poor working conditions; you may or may not agree with that idea.

To conclude, in my estimation, globalization is probably going to continue because capitalism has become the dominant world economic system. And capitalism in some form will continue to exist as long as people want newer, better, and more things than they have. The world is no longer like the Bhutan of forty years ago. Countries like China and India have a lesson for developing countries that rich countries either cannot or will not teach them. As Dani Rodrik so succinctly puts it: "Economic integration is the result, not the cause, of economic and social development." We are speaking here of the country's own economic and social development. Let me repeat that statement because it's important for you to take down: "Economic integration is the result, not the cause, of economic and social development." It may surprise you, but I am hopeful about the future, actually. I am thinking of a recent World Trade Organization meeting in Cancun, Mexico, where the world witnessed something that had never happened before. A group of twenty-three poorer nations came together and spoke with one voice. They spoke out against agricultural subsidies by rich countries, subsidies that make the poor countries' agricultural products less competitive in the world market. The twenty-three countries did not manage to abolish the subsidies at that meeting because the talks broke down. But there is a feeling that these countries have an awareness of their need to speak up for themselves—and hopefully to deal with richer nations on their own terms. If this means that they put the social and economic conditions of their own countries ahead of integrating into the world economy, they can only benefit. And perhaps the rich Western countries need to practice what they preach: how can they tell poor countries that tariffs and subsidies are bad when they use them extensively to protect their economies?

III. POSTLISTENING

A. Accuracy Check

1. Under globalization, do markets function nationally or internationally?

2. Does the lecturer see globalization as a cultural process or as an economic process?

3. Name two of the four groups that feel anger and mistrust toward globalization.

4. What do patents and copyright law often prevent poor countries from obtaining?

5. Name two non-Western countries that have integrated successfully into the world economy.

6. Did the four non-Western countries mentioned achieve economic progress in the same way or in different ways?

7. What two labor issues do critics of globalization bring up all the time?

8. Does the lecturer think globalization will exist in the future?

9. Is economic integration in the world economy the result—or the cause—of economic and social development in a country?

10. How many poor countries came together to speak out against agricultural subsidies at the Cancun WTO meeting?

| Unit Four | Education |

Chapter 10   Public Education: Philosophy and Funding

I. PRELISTENING

B. Vocabulary and Key Concepts

1. Education in the United States is <u>compulsory</u> until a certain age or grade level.

2. A small percentage of students attend private schools, either religious or <u>secular</u>, but most attend public schools.

3. There is no nationwide <u>curriculum</u>, nor are there nationwide <u>standardized</u> examinations set by the government.

4. The federal government influences public education by providing <u>funds</u> for special programs such as education for the <u>handicapped</u> and bilingual education.

5. Control of education in the United States is mainly <u>exercised locally</u>.

6. Each state has many school districts run by school boards whose members are <u>elected</u> by voters of the district.

7. The amount of funding supplied by the state and by the local school districts <u>fluctuates</u> over time and from state to state.

8. Public schools are funded to <u>a great degree</u> by local taxes.

9. Funding for private schools, which are generally religious schools, is now and has been <u>controversial</u> for some time.

10. Charter schools are <u>nonsectarian</u> public schools that <u>compete</u> with regular public schools for students.

11. Charter schools operate under <u>contract</u> to a sponsor, usually a state or local school board, to whom they are <u>accountable</u>.

12. <u>Supporters</u> of the voucher concept believe that private schools offer better education.

13. <u>Opponents</u> of the voucher concept claim that using tax money for private schools <u>violates</u> the separation of church and state built into the U.S. Constitution.

14. The federal government in 2002 passed an educational <u>bill</u> that requires states that wish to receive certain federal funding to develop and put in place extensive testing programs and other systems to ensure "<u>adequate yearly progress</u>" of students.

D. Notetaking Preparation

1. Structuring: Outlining
<script>

Control of education in the United States is mainly exercised locally at three levels. Let's begin with the state department of education. The department of education of each of the fifty states has two basic functions. First, each state department of education sets basic curriculum requirements for all the schools in its state. For example, a high school might require four years of English, three years of math, two years of social science, and so forth. The state also sets the number of credits a student must complete in order to graduate from a high school. This total number of credits includes both required courses and electives. So much for the state part in education.

The second level of control is the school district. The number of school districts a state has depends on the size of its population and the size of the state. A large metropolitan area would have several school districts. A smaller community might have only one district. Each school district is run by a school board that is elected by the citizens of the district. The school district is responsible for the specific content of courses taught in its schools. In other words, the school district determines what the students will study in each of their, let's say, four years of high school English. The school district also decides what electives will be available for students. Besides determining course content, the school district is responsible for the operation of the schools in its district, for example, the hiring of teachers and administrators. The third level of control is the individual school itself, where teachers have primary responsibility for deciding how to teach the content of each course and for preparing and giving examinations to the students.

II. LISTENING

LECTURE: Public Education: Philosophy and Funding

Most young people in the United States today, like most young people around the world, attend public schools. Indeed, young people in the U.S. have to attend school because education is compulsory, in most states to the age of sixteen or until the students reach ninth grade.

A small percentage of American youth attend private schools, either religious or secular schools, but the vast majority attend public schools. One distinguishing feature of U.S. public education that surprises many foreigners is that although there are some standardized examinations, there is no nationwide curriculum set by the government. Nor are there nationwide standardized examinations set by the government. In contrast, in most countries a government ministry of education determines the curriculum that all students study and the examinations that all students take at a set time. Of course, U.S. students follow a curriculum, and they take examinations as all students do. Although the federal government does influence public education by providing funds to schools for special programs such as education for the handicapped and for bilingual education, the federal government does not determine the curriculum or the examinations. Today I'd like to talk about the three levels of control within each state and then spend some time discussing where the money for education comes from and three issues related to funding.

Control of education in the United States is mainly exercised locally at three levels. Let's begin with the state department of education. The department of education of each of the fifty states has two basic functions. First, each state department of education sets basic curriculum requirements for all the schools in its state. For example, a high school might require four years of English, three years of math, two years of social science, and so forth. The state also sets the number of credits a student must complete in order to graduate from a high school. This total number of credits includes both required courses and electives. So much for the state part in education.

The second level of control is the school district. The number of school districts a state has depends on the size of its population and the size of the state. A large metropolitan area would have several school districts. A smaller community might have only one district. Each school district is run by a school board that is elected by the citizens of the district. The school district is responsible for the specific content of courses taught in its schools. In other words, the school district determines what the students will study in each of their, let's say, four years of high school English. The school district also decides what electives will be available for students. Besides determining course content, the school district is responsible for the operation of the schools in its district, for example, the hiring of teachers and administrators. The third level of control is the individual school itself, where teachers have primary responsibility for deciding how to teach the content of each course and for preparing and giving examinations to the students.

Local control of schools may seem very strange to some of you, but it will seem less strange if you consider how public schools in the United States are funded—that is, where money to run the schools comes from. Only about 7 percent of the money comes from the federal government. The rest of the money comes from state and local taxes. The percentages supplied by the state and by the local school districts fluctuate over time and from state to state. Currently approximately 49 percent of school funding comes from the states and about 44 percent comes from the local communities, that is, the school districts.

Finally, I'd like to discuss three issues related to the funding of schools that have been receiving a lot of attention recently in the United States. The first issue deals with the inequality of educational opportunity that students face. Because public schools are funded to a great degree by local taxes, this means that schools in poorer communities or poorer parts of large cities do not have the same amount of money as schools located in richer communities. This, in turn, means that children from poorer areas are less likely to receive a good education than children from wealthier areas. The second issue, one that has been controversial since the beginning of public education, is the issue of funding for private schools, which are generally run by religious organizations. As you already know, the First Amendment to the U.S. Constitution mandates separation of church and state. A little background on the history and development of public education will be useful here.

During colonial times, education was largely a religious concern and most schools were supported by religious organizations. However, during the nineteenth century, there was widespread support and acceptance of public education paid for by taxes as the best way to provide equal educational opportunity for all children. Nevertheless, some parents have always chosen to send their children to either private religious schools or private schools devoted to academic excellence. Because private schools are not funded by the government, parents have had to pay tuition to send their children to private schools. People who have wanted to send their children to private schools have long questioned why they should have to pay taxes for public schools at the same time as they pay private tuition for their children's education.

Although this issue is not new, during the last twenty years or so, more parents have become unhappy about what they perceive to be the increasingly secular nature of public education and prefer to send their children to schools where they will receive an education more in line with their religious beliefs. Other parents are concerned about the questionable quality of education in public schools. These concerns have led to efforts by the school system, and the government, to offer alternative educational opportunities, that is, educational choices. Two of the most important responses to these concerns have been charter schools and school vouchers. Both of these alternatives to regular public education are based on the idea that competition in the educational market is a good thing, but otherwise, they differ quite a bit.

Charter schools are nonsectarian public schools that compete with regular public schools for students. Charter schools operate under contract to a sponsor, usually a state or local school board. Charter schools are accountable to their sponsors, the parents who choose to send their children to them, and the public that funds them through their tax money. In turn, charter schools generally have greater autonomy, that is, independence, over selection of teachers, curriculum, resources, and so on, than regular public schools. The first charter schools came into existence toward the end of the 1980s. By 2003, there were 2,695 charter schools with almost 685,000 students enrolled. This was a 15 percent increase over the year 2002, which shows how fast these schools are growing. There are many issues surrounding charter schools, but a study published in 2003 found that charter school students did a little better than their public school counterparts on standardized exams.

The school voucher concept is a much more controversial one than charter schools. The idea behind school vouchers is that the government provides students with a certain amount of money each year that they can use to attend whatever school they choose, public or private. The idea again is that competition will improve the education students receive. Voucher schools in reality are largely private schools, and most often religiously based schools. They are quite different from charter schools, which as public schools are first of all, nonsectarian, that is, not religious. Second, charter schools cannot apply restrictive admission standards, as public schools do. To date, voucher programs funded by taxpayers are operating in only three U.S. cities, and there are many court battles over the voucher system. Supporters of the voucher system feel very strongly that private schools offer better education than public schools. Those opposed to the voucher system claim that vouchers rob public schools of needed funding and that voucher schools do not truly provide school choice because of restrictive admissions standards, which can include academic performance, religion, sex, and other factors. Opponents of vouchers also strongly believe that using taxpayer funds for private religious schools violates the separation of church and state built into the U.S. Constitution.

The third and final issue I'd like to touch on today is also very controversial. I mentioned earlier that the United States does not have a nationwide curriculum nor nationwide exams set by the government. However, in the past fifteen or twenty years, there has been an increased emphasis in various states on raising standards and on giving students standardized exams to monitor their progress. The federal government in 2002 passed a sweeping education bill that requires states that wish to receive certain federal funding to develop and put in place extensive testing programs and other systems to ensure adequate yearly progress of students. Although the percentage of funding for schools from the federal government is relatively small, it still represents a lot of money that schools do not want to lose. Some people support this movement toward standardization and accountability in the educational system, while others see it as a dangerous step away from local control of schools.

No one can predict the future of public education in the United States, but it appears that the emphasis on educational choice and on accountability of the educational system for student results will be with us for a long time.

III. POSTLISTENING

A. Accuracy Check

1. What two things about the American educational system often surprise people from other countries?

2. What are the three levels of control of education found in each state?

3. What is one type of decision that the state department of education might make?

4. How are the people on a school board selected?

5. From what three sources does the money come to pay for American public schools, and what percentage of that money comes from each of these three sources?

6. During the colonial period, who generally ran the schools that children attended?

7. During which century did public education paid for by taxes become widely accepted as the best way to provide education for all children?

8. What do we call nonsectarian public schools that operate quite independently under contract, usually to a school district?

9. What kind of schools do students with vouchers usually attend?

10. How do opponents of the movement toward standardized exams and accountability view this movement?

Chapter 11   Postsecondary Education: Admissions

I. PRELISTENING

B. Vocabulary and Key Concepts

1. <u>Postsecondary</u> education in the United States includes <u>community</u> as well as four-year colleges, most of which are <u>coeducational</u>.

2. To be <u>accredited</u>, a college must meet certain <u>standards</u> set by institutional and professional associations.

3. The more <u>prestigious</u> private schools are more <u>competitive</u>—that is, they have stiffer admissions requirements.

4. All college applicants must submit a <u>transcript</u> of high school grades and often <u>standardized</u> test results.

5. A student's <u>extracurricular</u> activities and possibly <u>ethnic</u> <u>background</u> are often factors in his or her admission.

6. Among the 2.8 million high school graduates in 2002, 65.2 percent <u>were</u> <u>enrolled</u> in college the following October.

7. If we <u>break</u> <u>down</u> the statistics racially, we find that white students enrolled in college in greater <u>proportions</u> than black or Hispanic students.

8. They may be people who attend part-time to <u>upgrade</u> their <u>skills</u>, people who are changing careers, or retired people who still have a desire to learn.

9. Because most young American students have not traveled in other countries, they are not very <u>well</u> <u>versed</u> in international matters, and foreign students often find them friendly but not very <u>well</u> <u>informed</u> about their countries or cultures.

10. Some students begin college at a community college with more <u>lenient</u> admissions requirements and later <u>transfer</u> to a four-year college.

D. Notetaking Preparation

1. Structuring: Listening
   <script>

An interesting feature of education in the United States is the community college. Community colleges that are publicly supported offer somewhat different educational opportunities than those offered by a senior college or a university. First, admissions requirements at public community colleges are usually much more lenient than those at a four-year college or university. It's usually enough to have graduated from an American high school to be admitted. Second, it is also cheaper to attend a community college. The tuition and fees are usually quite a bit lower. Students often live at home because this type of school does not have dormitories. For these two reasons, many people who are unable to go to a four-year college or university can have an opportunity to take classes for college credit. Finally, community colleges offer two-year programs that can lead to an Associate of Arts degree. Many of these programs, but not all of them, are vocational in nature. In conclusion, people attend community colleges for many different purposes. Some people may be taking only a course or two in some field that particularly interests them and may not be planning on getting a degree. Other people may be going to community college full-time and planning to transfer to a four-year college or university upon successful completion of two years at a community college.

II. LISTENING

LECTURE: Postsecondary Education: Admissions

In this lecture, I'm going to talk to you about postsecondary education in the United States. Today I'll give you some facts and figures about colleges and universities in the United States and some general information about admissions policies. I will also make a few remarks about community colleges and finish up by giving you an idea of what kinds of students make up the student body on a typical U.S. campus.

Let's begin with some facts and figures. The most recent figures I have reveal there are 4,182 public and private four-year and two-year colleges in the United States. These range from full universities with diverse programs to smaller four-year colleges to two-year community colleges. Most of them are accredited, which means the schools meet certain standards set by institutional and private evaluators. When applying to a school, you would probably want to make sure it was accredited. Even though there are more private colleges than public ones, over three-quarters of students, precisely 78 percent, are enrolled at public colleges and universities. Some of the small private schools may have fewer than 100 students, whereas some of the large state university systems may have 50,000 or more students. Most of these schools are coeducational although some of them are primarily for women and others are primarily for men. Some schools may offer only one program of study and others have a great variety of programs. The total cost for attending one of these schools may be less than $5,000 a year or as much as 30 or 40 thousand dollars a year for one of the prestigious private schools. These schools are located all over—in industrial areas, agricultural areas, large cities, and small towns in a wide variety of climates.

With such a wide variety of sizes, kinds, and locations of schools, it probably won't surprise you to find out that admissions requirements at these colleges and universities vary greatly also. Some are relatively easy to be admitted to whereas others are highly competitive. However, most schools will ask undergraduate applicants to submit their high school transcripts with a record of their grades and test results from one of the standardized tests regularly offered to high school students. The most common of these standardized exams is the Scholastic Aptitude Test, commonly known as the SAT. Students who are applying to graduate school are usually asked to take other, more specific standardized exams depending on which college they are applying to. For example, some students are required to take the Graduate Record Exam, or the GRE. Students applying to a business college will probably have to take the GMAT, and students applying to law college will have to take the LSAT. You probably know about the TOEFL exam, which most foreign students have to take before being admitted to American colleges or universities. These exams, including the TOEFL, are all prepared by a company that is independent of the school system. These exams have come under a lot of criticism lately, but they are still widely used as one way to determine who will be admitted to various schools. However, most schools try to look at the whole student and consider factors other than simply grades and test scores. Some of these factors may be extracurricular activities in school, ethnic background, work experience, and so on. Some schools will have personal interviews with students they are considering for admission. Many schools, private as well as public, try very hard to have a student population with a wide variety of backgrounds and ages. Even the most prestigious and most highly competitive colleges and universities will not take only those students with the highest grades and standardized test scores but will consider these other factors. Nevertheless, schools of this type, such as Stanford and Harvard, have so many more people applying than they can possibly accept that students who want to get into such schools take grades and SAT exams very seriously. In general, medical and law colleges, both private and public, are very difficult to get into, and, once again, test scores on standardized exams can be extremely important to those applying to these schools.

However, for students who want to attend a state college or university in their own state, it may be enough to graduate from high school in the upper third or even upper half of their high school class. This may surprise those of you who come from an educational system that is highly competitive, a system in which only a small percentage of students who pass a very difficult nationwide standardized high school examination can enter a university. You may be even more surprised by what I have to tell you about community colleges.

An interesting feature of education in the United States is the two-year community college. Community colleges that are publicly supported offer somewhat different educational opportunities than those offered by a senior college or a university. First, admissions requirements at public community colleges are usually much more lenient than those at a four-year college or university. It's usually enough to have graduated from an American high school to be admitted. Second, it is also cheaper to attend a community college. The tuition and fees are usually quite a bit lower. Students often live at home because this type of school does not have dormitories. For these two reasons, many people who are unable to go to a four-year college or university can have an opportunity to take classes for college credit. Finally, community colleges offer two-year programs that can lead to an Associate of Arts degree. Many of these programs, but not all of them, are vocational in nature. People attend community colleges for many different purposes. Some people may be taking only a course or two in some field that particularly interests them and may not be planning on getting a degree. Other people may be going to community college full-time and planning to transfer to a four-year college or university upon successful completion of two years at a community college. Well, so much for community colleges.

I promised to tell you a little about the actual student body on a typical U.S. campus. Let's start with some statistics, and then we'll discuss two items that surprise many foreign students. Among the 2.8 million high school graduates in 2002, 65.2 percent were enrolled in college the following October. More than 90 percent of those attended full time. Young men represented half of the high school graduates, but more women than men went on to college. The exact statistics are: 68.4 percent of female high school graduates and 62.1 percent of male high school graduates. If we break down the statistics racially, we find that white students enrolled in college in greater proportions than black or Hispanic students. The figures are 66.7 percent of white graduates, 58.7 percent of black graduates, and 53.5 percent of Hispanic students. My next statistic may be surprising. 42.6 percent of full-time students in 2002 were either employed or looking for work. That number jumps to 75.7 percent for part-time students. That last statistic makes more sense when we consider that besides the students who are from eighteen to twenty-two years old that one expects to find on a college campus, there are also many older married students. They may be people who attend part-time to upgrade their skills, people who are changing careers, or retired people who still have a desire to learn. Also, foreign students are often surprised at how poorly prepared American students are when they enter a university. Actually, at very select schools the students are usually very well prepared, but at less selective schools, they may not be as well prepared as students in your country are. If you will remember the educational philosophy we discussed in the last lecture, you will understand why. Schools in the States simply admit a lot more students than is usual in most other countries. Also, most young American university students have not traveled in other countries and are not very well versed in international matters and do not know a lot about people from other countries. Foreign students usually find them friendly but not very well informed about their countries or cultures.

In brief, you can see that educational opportunities and admissions standards vary greatly in the United States. While it may be quite difficult to gain admission to some colleges and universities because of the very large number of applicants, probably any student graduating from high school with reasonable grades can find some accredited university or college to attend. Those students hoping to enter graduate school will often face very stiff competition, whether at private or public schools. Many students who start at a college or university will not finish in four years. Some will drop out to work or travel and may never finish. Others will return to school a few months or a few years later. Some will go to school full-time and others part-time. Some will not work while going to school, but most will work at some time or other during their school years.

We're out of time, I see. In my next lecture, I'll talk to you about a relatively new development in education, distance learning. It should be of interest to those of you who want to attend college but can't because of living far from a college, busy schedules, or for other reasons.

III. POSTLISTENING

A. Accuracy Check

1. How many public and private four-year and two-year colleges are there in the United States?

2. How many students do these individual colleges and universities have?

3. What is the range of tuition at one of these colleges?

4. What two kinds of academic records will most undergraduate colleges or universities ask applicants to submit?

5. What are two examples of the names of standardized tests that graduate students may have to take before being admitted to a graduate program?

6. What are two examples of nonacademic factors that a U.S. college or university might consider before admitting a student?

7. What are three ways that community colleges are generally different from senior colleges and universities?

8. What kind of a degree can a student get from a community college?

9. What percentage of high school graduates in 2002 were enrolled in college the following October?

10. What percentage of full-time college students were employed in 2002?

I. PRELISTENING

B. Vocabulary and Key Concepts

1. Can you imagine getting a college, or university, degree without ever once <u>setting</u> <u>foot</u> on a college campus?

2. "Distance education is <u>instruction</u> that occurs when the instructor and student are <u>separated</u> by distance or time, or both."

3. As early as 1840, it was possible to take a <u>correspondence</u> course in shorthand.

4. *Peterson's 1994 Guide to Distance Learning* listed ninety-three <u>accredited</u> distance education programs available at <u>community</u> colleges and universities across the United States and Canada.

5. First, rapidly changing economic conditions require many professional people to <u>upgrade</u> their knowledge or skills on an almost <u>continuous</u> basis.

6. At the same time that the demand for postsecondary education is growing, many U.S. colleges and universities are facing <u>budget</u> <u>crunches</u>.

7. Millions of people have <u>access</u> to audio, video, and computer <u>technology</u>.

8. The <u>modes</u> of instruction can <u>vary</u> greatly.

9. CD-ROMs may come to the student <u>via</u> <u>mail</u> or the student may <u>download</u> materials from the Internet.

10. Many distance education programs have a <u>residency</u> requirement.

11. The <u>dropout</u> rate from distance education courses and programs is higher than for <u>traditional</u> courses and programs.

12. There are many <u>unscrupulous</u> and disreputable universities advertising on the Internet with very <u>alluring</u> Web sites.

13. It is important for anyone wishing to take a course or to pursue a degree to check out the <u>credentials</u> of the school they are considering very carefully.

II. LISTENING

LECTURE: Distance Education

One of the most exciting changes in education in the United States today is the incredible growth of distance education at the post–secondary level. Let me begin the lecture by asking you a couple of questions. First, can you imagine getting a college, or university, degree, without ever once setting foot on a college campus? Second, would you believe me if I told you there are a few higher education institutions that grant degrees that don't even have a campus? Some of these schools even grant graduate degrees, that is, a master's degree or even a Ph.D.

What is distance education? A publication called *Distance Education: A Consumer's Guide* defines distance education this way: "Distance education is instruction that occurs when the instructor and student are separated by distance or time, or both." That sounds a little strange, but it's not really new.

As early as 1840, it was possible to take a correspondence course in shorthand; that is, a student could learn shorthand by mail. And the University of Wisconsin offered the first correspondence catalog in 1892. This meant that a student could take university courses by mail over 100 years ago. So distance education is not really new; however, modern technology, such as audio, video, and computer technology, has changed distance education a great deal. Today almost all distance education programs are online or have an online learning component to take advantage of the technology.

As I mentioned, distance education is now growing at an incredible rate. *Peterson's 1994 Guide to Distance Learning* listed 93 accredited distance education programs available at community colleges and universities across the United States and Canada, whereas its 1997 guide listed more than 700 programs. In 2003, almost 1,100 programs were listed. According to the U.S. Department of State, more than 90 percent of all accredited U.S. colleges and universities with 10,000 students or more offer distance education programs with new ones coming online continuously.

Distance education is quite a complex subject with many aspects to look at. Today let's look at the reasons why distance education is growing so rapidly, how distance education works, that is, what the modes of delivery are, and some things people considering distance education need to be aware of.

To start with, why is distance education growing at such an incredible rate?

First, rapidly changing economic conditions require many professional people to upgrade their knowledge or skills on an almost continuous basis. For example, a person who graduates with a degree in engineering or computer science may find it necessary to take courses to upgrade his or her skills every few years. Or a person who begins his or her career with a B.A. or B.S. degree may find it desirable to pursue an M.A. after some time, or even a Ph.D. Busy working people often find it difficult or even impossible to take the courses they need or to pursue degrees on campus. Thus, there are a lot of people wanting postsecondary education who don't find it convenient to study in the traditional on-campus setting.

At the same time that the demand for postsecondary education is growing, many U.S. colleges and universities are facing budget crunches; that is, they just don't have as much money as they had in the past, but at the same time they have more students. They have to find ways to deliver instruction in the most economical way possible.

The final reason is modern technology, which is the key to making the desired postsecondary education available to the millions of people who have access to audio, video, and computer technology.

Many institutions offer distance education courses, certificate programs, and degree programs. How does distance education work at the postsecondary level? What are the usual modes of delivery?

The modes of instruction can vary greatly and different courses in a program may use different modes. And any given course may use several different modes. Some of the modes include video, audio, CD-ROM, Internet, bulletin boards, chat rooms, and e-mail. Let's consider some of the possibilities among these technologies. Video, for example, can be as simple as videotape the student plays on his or her VCR. Or it could involve video conferencing where the student is able to see and interact with the instructor and other students. Audio works similarly. A student may have a set of audiotapes to play on a cassette player or may be connected to an audio conference where he or she interacts with other students and the instructor. When students study on their own, at a time convenient to them, from a video- or audiotape, it is asynchronous learning, asynchronous meaning not at the same time. Video and audio conferencing, on the other hand, are called synchronous learning; that is, the instructor and the students are engaged in the teaching and learning process at the same time. Let's look at two other popular modes used in distance learning: bulletin boards and chat rooms. Both provide a place for discussion among students taking the same course. A student can log on to a bulletin board anytime of the day and night, read what other students have written, and respond, by either adding his or her ideas or asking a question. Chat rooms, on the other hand, offer a discussion forum where students can interact in real time, that is, synchronously. CD-ROMs may come to the student via mail or the student may download materials from the Internet. E-mail provides a very convenient way for students to submit assignments or to ask the instructor questions. There are many more modes of instruction, but this should give you an idea of the possibilities.

Students interested in pursuing distance education degrees need to consider the following six points:

Number 1. Many distance education programs have a residency requirement. The students may be required to take two courses on campus, that is, six hours of credit, or students may be required to spend several days on campus several times during the program.

Number 2. Distance education courses generally have time limits. Courses and programs must be completed within a certain time limit. Assignments must be submitted on time.

Number 3. Admissions requirements are the same as those of an on-campus education.

Number 4. Distance education can save students money in terms of not having to travel to campus for classes, and the like, but the academic fees are about the same as for traditional education. Fulfilling the residency requirements may be quite costly in terms of travel and lodging for students who live far from the campus.

Number 5. Online study requires students to have access to a computer that meets minimum requirements such as the latest version of Windows, a microphone, sound card and speakers, adequate hard drive and RAM, a modem, browser (Internet Explorer or Netscape), and Internet connection. Connection speed is very important and many schools recommend having high-speed Internet access like a cable modem or DSL.

And finally Number 6. Distance learning requires that students be disciplined and independent learners. Distance education is not easier than traditional education. Not everyone is temperamentally suited for distance education. The dropout rate from distance education courses and programs is higher than for traditional courses and programs.

Before I close today, let me just say that many people are still suspicious of distance education believing that it cannot possibly be equivalent to a traditional classroom education, although there are studies that indicate that distance education can be as effective as traditional education and sometimes even more effective. However, some suspicions are well founded. There are many unscrupulous and disreputable universities advertising on the Internet with very alluring Web sites. Therefore, it is important for anyone wishing to take a course or to pursue a degree to check out the credentials of the school they are considering very carefully.

We have an expression: Let the buyer beware. That means that anyone who wishes to buy something should be very careful! And that includes online or distance education.

III. POSTLISTENING

A. Accuracy Check

1. In what two ways can the instructor and student be separated in distance education?

2. How could students learn shorthand in 1840 without having to attend classes?

3. In what year was the first university correspondence catalog offered in the United States?

4. According to the U.S. Department of State, what percentage of accredited U.S. colleges and universities with 10,000 or more students offer distance education programs?

5. What does the term <u>synchronous</u> mean?

6. Name three modes of delivery of instruction used in distance education.

7. Can students take all the time they want or need to complete distance education courses or programs?

8. Are the fees for distance education programs generally cheaper than those for traditional on-campus programs?

9. What are two ways many schools recommend that students get high-speed Internet access?

10. Do students complete distance education courses and programs at the same rate as traditional courses and programs?

Unit Five | The Official Side

Chapter 13   The Role of Government in the Economy

I. PRELISTENING

B. Vocabulary and Key Concepts

1. One of the important characteristics of American-style capitalism is individual <u>ownership</u> of <u>property</u>, including such things as houses and land, businesses, and intellectual property such as songs, poems, books, and inventions.

2. The second characteristic is <u>free enterprise</u>.

3. The idea in a pure capitalistic system is for the government not to <u>interfere</u>, that is, for the government to take a <u>laissez-faire</u> attitude.

4. In a pure capitalistic system, the government's role would be severely limited. It would be responsible only for laws governing <u>contracts</u> and property, as well as for the <u>national</u> <u>defense</u>.

5. Companies may have to install pollution <u>control</u> equipment to <u>comply with</u> government regulations.

6. People who earn little or no <u>income</u> can receive <u>public</u> <u>assistance</u>, often called <u>welfare</u>.

7. The government makes sure that the marketplace stays <u>competitive</u> through its <u>antitrust</u> and <u>monopoly</u> laws.

8. The government interferes with the economy in an effort to maintain <u>stability</u>.

9. Through <u>taxation</u>, the government tries to control <u>inflation</u>.

10. The government has to be very careful to keep <u>unemployment</u> and inflation in <u>balance</u>, however.

11. The government further tries to achieve stability through its <u>expenditures</u> and by controlling the <u>interest</u> rate.

12. Republicans, the more <u>conservative</u> party, tend to <u>favor</u> fewer taxes, less welfare to the poor, and conditions that help business grow.

13. The government's role in the economy is not a <u>static</u> thing because the <u>composition</u> of the government changes every few years.

II. LISTENING

LECTURE: The Role of Government in the Economy

Let me begin today by saying that the American economy is basically a capitalistic economy. One of the important characteristics of American-style capitalism is individual ownership of property, including such things as houses and land, businesses, and intellectual property such as songs, poems, books, and inventions. The second characteristic is free enterprise. This means the freedom to produce, buy, and sell goods and labor without government intervention. The third characteristic is free competitive markets. Those businesses that succeed stay in the market, and those that fail must leave the market. In this type of economy, not everyone will be able to find a job at every moment and not all businesses will be successful, but in a pure capitalistic system, the government is not expected to interfere with the natural economic forces. The idea in a pure capitalistic system is for the government to take a laissez-faire attitude toward business.

Thus, in a purely capitalistic society the government's role would be limited to a very few areas. For example, the government would make laws concerning contracts and property rights. The government would also be responsible for national defense. Finally, in a pure capitalist state the government would provide only those goods that private businesses could or would not ordinarily provide, such as roads and canals.

In truth, because the United States is not a pure capitalistic system, government today does not maintain a completely laissez-faire attitude toward business. The government's role in business has been growing since the beginning of the century, especially since the 1930s. This expanding role of government is another complicated subject, and I'm going to discuss only a few issues today, just to give you some idea of why the government tries to regulate the economy. We'll be discussing four basic reasons for government interference.

The first reason the government tries to regulate the economy is to protect the environment. Because the costs of polluting the environment can affect all members of society, the government uses various legal means to try to regulate businesses and to protect the environment. Companies must comply with certain government regulations. For example, companies may be required to install expensive pollution control equipment. The government also has regulations about how and where toxic wastes can be dumped and imposes fines upon those companies that do not follow these regulations.

The second reason the government interferes with the economy is to help people who for some reason beyond their control earn little or no income. These people may be too young or too old or too ill or otherwise unable to support themselves. The government has various public assistance, or welfare programs, that are paid for with tax money to help these people.

The third reason the government interferes in the economy is to try to see that the marketplace stays competitive. Early in the century the government passed antitrust and monopoly regulation laws. Antitrust laws were passed to prevent businesses from joining together to drive other businesses out of the marketplace. Monopoly regulation laws were designed to prevent a situation where one business, because of its size and strength, just naturally drove all other similar businesses out of the marketplace. The government believed that it was better to interfere in the economy to be sure that competition was protected. The government still enforces these laws today. For example, the government forced the telephone company, a giant monopoly, to split up into smaller companies. This allowed other companies to enter the market and compete with these smaller companies instead of having one giant monopoly.

The last reason for the government's interfering with the economy is to maintain economic stability. Basically, the government uses three methods to achieve stability. The first is taxation, by which the government collects money from people and businesses. The second method used to keep the economy stable is through expenditure, the money that the government spends. And the third method the government uses to maintain stability is controlling the interest rate on money it lends to businesses. Let's look at each of these methods in more detail. First, let's look at how the government uses taxation to stabilize the economy. If the economy is growing too fast, inflation becomes a problem. The government can raise taxes to take money out of the economy and lower the inflation rate. However, raising taxes can also lead to increased unemployment. Therefore, the government has to be very careful to regulate taxes to keep unemployment and inflation in balance. The second way the government promotes stability is through its own expenditure, as I just mentioned. The government has a huge amount of money to spend every year. Some of its decisions about how to spend the money are based on economic conditions in different industries or in different parts of the country. For example, the government may try to help the economy of a certain state by buying goods and services from businesses inside that state.

And a third way is by controlling the interest rate on the money the government will lend to business. If the economy is growing too slowly, the government lowers the interest rate. The lowering of the interest rate will encourage individuals to borrow more money to begin new businesses and expand old businesses. If the government feels that the economy is growing too fast, the government raises the interest rate. Raising the interest rate will discourage investment in new businesses and business expansion. These three ways, taxation, expenditure, and setting the interest rate, are the government's main means of maintaining the economy's stability.

Generally speaking, the two major political parties in the United States differ on how big a role they think the government should play in the economy. Republicans, the more conservative party, tend to favor fewer taxes, less welfare to the poor, and conditions that help business grow. Democrats, on the other hand, are often more protective of the environment and more sympathetic to the needs of the old, poor, and sick. Democrats are, consequently, more often in favor of raising taxes to pay for social programs and of regulating businesses more closely. The government's role in the economy is not a static thing because the composition of the government can change every few years. So, the extent to which the government interferes in the economy changes depending on which party the president is from, which party has a majority in Congress, and how well the president and Congress work together. But I am getting close to the topic of the next lecture, so I'll stop here.

III. POSTLISTENING

A. Accuracy Check

1. What are two examples of intellectual property?

2. What does free enterprise mean?

3. What are two examples of the kinds of things the government would be responsible for in a pure capitalistic system?

4. Does the lecturer suggest that the role of the government in the economy is greater or less in this century than it was in the last century?

5. What is the government's role in relation to the environment?

6. For what kinds of reasons are some people not able to earn enough money to take care of themselves?

7. Does the lecturer suggest that the government thinks competition is a good or bad thing?

8. What is an example of a large American company that was forced to divide itself into many smaller companies?

9. What are the three methods that the government uses to maintain economic stability?

10. When the economy is growing too fast, does the government raise or lower the interest rate on money it lends to business?

Chapter 14 · Government by Constitution

I. PRELISTENING

B. Vocabulary and Key Concepts

1. Two important principles of the U.S. Constitution are the <u>division</u> of powers and the system of <u>checks</u> and <u>balances</u>.

2. The Constitution provides for three <u>branches</u> of government: the <u>legislative</u>, the executive, and the <u>judicial</u>.

3. The legislative branch is primarily responsible for <u>enacting</u>, or making, new laws. The executive branch executes laws by signing them and by seeing that they are <u>enforced</u>.

4. The judicial branch deals with those who are <u>accused</u> <u>of</u> <u>breaking</u> a law or who are involved in a <u>legal</u> <u>dispute</u>.

5. The judicial branch also handles <u>trials</u> and reviews existing laws to make sure they are <u>consistent</u> <u>with</u> the U.S. Constitution.

6. Each branch has its specific <u>tasks</u> and its own particular power, which it must not <u>abuse</u>.

7. The presidential <u>power</u> <u>of</u> <u>veto</u> is an obvious example of checks and balances.

8. Because it's difficult for Congress to <u>override</u> a presidential veto, the veto may <u>put</u> <u>an</u> <u>end</u> <u>to</u> this new law forever.

9. Although President Nixon was <u>suspected</u> of illegal activities, he was never removed from office by Congress because he <u>resigned</u>.

10. By finding laws against abortion <u>unconstitutional</u>, the Supreme Court in effect made abortion <u>legal</u>.

11. In the area of <u>civil</u> <u>rights</u>, the Supreme Court declared it illegal to practice <u>racial</u> <u>discrimination</u> in any form.

12. Probably the most important effect of this change was the <u>desegregation</u> of public schools.

13. After the president <u>nominates</u> <u>a</u> <u>candidate</u> for the Supreme Court, the Congress must <u>approve</u> his choice.

14. Because there are only nine Supreme Court Justices, one new Justice can change the <u>balance</u> <u>of</u> <u>power</u> on the Court itself.

II. LISTENING

LECTURE: Government by Constitution: Separation of Powers/Checks and Balances

The year 1987 marked the 200th anniversary of the U.S. Constitution. We all know that the United States is a comparatively young country, but the interesting thing is that its constitution is the oldest written one that has been in continuous use. For over 200 years, it has provided the basis for a stable government and has remained basically unchanged. Today we will try to understand the U.S. government better by looking at two important principles provided by the Constitution. These two principles so important to understanding the U.S. government were written into the Constitution 200 years ago and are still in effect today. These two principles are (1) the division, or separation, of power; and (2) a system of checks and balances. Before we begin our discussion of these two principles, let's first take a look at the three branches that compose the U.S. government.

To start, the Constitution provides for three branches of government. These three branches are (1) the legislative, (2) the executive, and (3) the judicial. First, the legislative branch, which is the Congress of the United States, is primarily responsible for enacting, or making, new laws that are to be followed by the fifty states of the country. Second, the executive branch, which is headed by the president, executes these same laws that originate in the legislature. By signing the laws, the president actually puts the laws into effect. After the president has signed a new law, the executive branch of the government is also responsible for seeing that the new law is enforced, or carried out. Well, these are the first two branches, so we're ready to discuss the third branch. Do you recall what the third branch is? You're right if you said the judicial. What do you think the judicial branch does? Well, the judicial branch is primarily responsible for dealing with persons or corporations that are accused of breaking a law or that are involved in any kind of legal dispute. The judicial system also handles trials and other types of court cases. Another very important responsibility of the judicial branch is to review existing laws to make sure that they are consistent with the U.S. Constitution. In other words, the judicial branch must judge the legality of laws, using the Constitution as a guide.

You already have an idea of what is meant by division of powers from the preceding discussion. Each branch of the government has its specific task in relation to the country's laws. Each branch has its own particular power, then, that is not shared by the other two branches. This division of power was intended by the writers of the Constitution to make sure that no single branch of the government could ever have all the power. And what's more, to make sure that no single branch could abuse its power or become more powerful than the other two branches, a system of checks and balances was written into the Constitution. This system of checks and balances gives each branch of the government a specific way to check, or keep some control on, each of the other branches. The best way to understand this system of checks and balances might be to discuss a few examples of how it works.

First, let's consider how the executive branch can check the power of the legislative branch. The most obvious example is the presidential power of veto. Suppose the president feels that a law enacted by Congress is unwise. If he feels very strongly that this new law is wrong, he may refuse to sign it. Now Congress can override a presidential veto, but it is a very difficult thing to do, so a presidential veto may put an end to this new law forever. Now let's look at an example of how the legislative branch, or Congress, may check the power of the executive branch. Many of you will have heard of the Watergate scandal, which took place in Washington, DC, in 1973. In the Watergate affair, President Richard Nixon and his staff were suspected of illegal actions to re-elect Nixon. In such a case, where the executive branch is suspected of illegal or unconstitutional activities, the legislative branch is given the power by the Constitution to investigate these activities. If Congress believes that illegal activities have actually taken place, it has the power to remove the president from office. This, in fact, did not happen to President Nixon because he resigned, but steps to investigate the legality of his actions had already been initiated by Congress at the time that he resigned. For two more examples of checks and balances, let's take a look at two instances in which the judicial branch checked, or limited, the power of the legislative branch. The first example concerns the legality of abortion. Some years ago, most states in the United States had laws that made abortion illegal. In reviewing these laws in 1973, the U.S. Supreme Court, which is the highest authority in the judicial branch, found these laws unconstitutional. By finding these laws unconstitutional, the Supreme Court in effect made abortion legal; therefore, women have the right to obtain an abortion in all fifty states today. Our next example concerns civil rights. The Supreme Court declared unconstitutional state laws that discriminated against African Americans. As a result, it became illegal for any state to practice racial discrimination in any form. Probably the most important effect of this change was the desegregation of the public schools. These are some examples of how the judicial branch checks the power of the legislative branch. These two examples concern state laws, but the Supreme Court also reviews and determines the constitutionality of federal laws originated in Congress, so you can see how powerful the Supreme Court really is. You might wonder what check the executive or the legislative branch has on the judicial branch. Well, first of all, the president is the person who nominates the candidates for the Supreme Court. After the president nominates a candidate, Congress must approve the choice. Because there are only nine Supreme Court Justices, the opportunity to nominate even one candidate for the Supreme Court is an opportunity to change the balance of power on the Court itself. Any candidate nominated for the Supreme Court by the president can expect to be questioned very extensively by members of Congress about his or her record on such issues as abortion, gun control, separation of church and state, and so on, depending on current political concerns in the country. Under the Constitution, each branch of the government, then, must answer to the other two branches. Therefore, ideally, no one branch can exercise too much power or abuse the power that it has. From time to time, one branch of the government appears to be quite a bit more powerful than one or both of the other branches, but this imbalance of power does not usually last a long time. In the long run, each branch guards its own power quite vigorously, and all three branches check and balance one another's power.

III. POSTLISTENING

A. Accuracy Check

1. How is the U.S. Constitution different from all other constitutions in the world?

2. What are the three branches of the U.S. government?

3. What is the responsibility of the executive branch of the government?

4. Who is the head of the executive branch of the government?

5. What is meant by checks and balances?

6. What is meant by the veto power of the president?

7. What normally happens if the president vetoes a law?

8. How can the legislative branch of government, or the Congress, check the power of the executive branch?

9. What might have happened to President Nixon had he not resigned?

10. How does the legislative branch have an opportunity to check the power of the judicial branch?

I. PRELISTENING

B. Vocabulary and Key Concepts

1. The average person in the legal profession would probably say it's better to let a dozen <u>guilty</u> people go free than to punish one innocent person <u>unjustly</u>.

2. The guiding principle for the U.S. legal system is that an accused person is <u>innocent</u> <u>until</u> <u>proven</u> <u>guilty</u>.

3. Under civil law, the judge consults a complex <u>code</u> <u>of</u> <u>laws</u> to decide whether the defendant is guilty and, if so, what sentence to give.

4. Under <u>common</u> <u>law</u>, the judge considers the <u>precedents</u> set by other court decisions.

5. The jury hears <u>testimony</u> in either civil or criminal trials and reaches a <u>verdict</u>.

6. A civil trial is one that deals with disputes between <u>private</u> <u>parties</u>, often involving contracts or property rights.

7. In a civil trial, the jury decides which side is right and how much money should be paid in <u>compensatory</u> and <u>punitive</u> <u>damages</u>.

8. For a jury to convict a person in a criminal case, they must believe the person guilty "<u>beyond</u> <u>a</u> <u>reasonable</u> <u>doubt</u>."

9. A person's liberty and even life can be taken away if he or she is <u>convicted</u>, that is, found guilty, of a crime.

10. Some of a judge's responsibilities are excluding <u>irrelevant</u> remarks and questions by lawyers and witnesses and deciding what kind of <u>evidence</u> is <u>admissible</u>.

11. If the required number of jurors cannot agree on a decision, it is called a <u>hung</u> jury, and the law requires a new trial.

12. What happens in plea bargaining is that the accused <u>pleads</u> <u>guilty</u> to a <u>lesser</u> <u>crime</u>.

II. LISTENING

LECTURE: Common Law and the Jury System

The legal system of a country—that is, its system of justice—reflects the history and culture of the country just as much as other topics we have discussed so far. When we start to discuss law, courts, trials, and concepts of innocence and guilt, there are some broad philosophical questions that come up, questions that might be interesting to think about before talking more about the legal system in the United States. Because people from different cultures might answer these questions differently, let's take a few minutes and see how you would answer these for your country.

Now, the first question: Is it preferable for a dozen guilty people to go free rather than to punish one innocent person unjustly? Or is it sometimes necessary to punish innocent people so that no guilty person escapes justice? Here's the other question for you: Is a person guilty until he is proven innocent? Or does it seem more logical to you that he is innocent until he is proven guilty?

I suspect that the average person in the legal profession in the United States would say that it is better to let a dozen guilty people go free rather than to punish one innocent person unjustly. In addition, the guiding principle for the U.S. legal system is that an accused person is innocent until proven guilty. Now that you've had a chance to think about these two philosophical questions, let's look at the U.S. legal system in terms of what makes it different from legal systems in many other countries. First, we'll look at U.S. common law and how it differs from civil law as practiced in many countries in the world. Then we'll look more closely at the jury system, a system that many foreigners find quite curious. Then, if there's time, I'd like to make a few concluding remarks about plea bargaining—the way that most cases, in fact, are settled out of court. I think, then, that you'll be able to get a feeling for how the United States' approach to law is different from that in your country.

To begin with, the U.S. system of justice is not unique. We have to remember that it is a system brought over by the first settlers from England. At that time, there were two basic legal systems in Europe, common law as practiced in Great Britain and civil law as practiced in other European countries. To simplify greatly, civil law depends on a written code of laws. In deciding a case, under civil law the judge consults this code, a complex set of written laws, to decide whether the defendant is innocent or guilty and, if guilty, what sentence the defendant will be given. On the other hand, common law, generally practiced in English-speaking countries including the United States, has developed case by case. Besides considering written law to determine the defendant's guilt, under common law the judge also considers the precedent set by other court decisions. In deciding a case under common law, then, the judge looks at what other judges have decided in similar cases in the past. So the judge is guided *not only* by a legal code but also by previous court decisions. And very often, it is not the judge who brings a verdict under the common law but the jury.

The U.S. Constitution guarantees the right to trial by jury. A jury is a group of six to twelve ordinary citizens. The jury hears testimony in either civil or criminal trials and reaches a verdict. A civil trial is one that deals with disputes between private parties, often involving contracts or property rights. Criminal trials are ones where the government, representing the public, prosecutes those accused of a crime. In a civil trial, the jury decides which side is right and how much money should be paid in damages. In a criminal trial, the jury decides guilt or innocence. There are two other big differences between criminal and civil trials. First, the defendant in a criminal case does not have to testify. It is the government's job to show guilt, not the defendant's job to prove innocence. In a civil trial, the defendant must testify. Second, for a jury to convict a person in a criminal case, they must believe the person guilty "beyond a reasonable doubt." The government must present a high degree of proof. The jury in a civil trial decides which side has presented more evidence to support its case. This is a lower degree of proof than "reasonable doubt." The reason that the degree of proof is much higher in a criminal trial is that a person's liberty and even life can be taken away if he or she is convicted, that is, found guilty, of a crime.

The judge at a trial and the jury have very different responsibilities. The judge's main responsibility is to see that the trial is conducted according to the law. Part of this responsibility is excluding irrelevant remarks and questions by lawyers and witnesses and deciding what kind of evidence is admissible. The jury, on the other hand, decide whether they believe the testimony they hear and whether the evidence presented to them is valid.

Some of you may remember the trial of the American former football star O. J. Simpson for the murder of his ex-wife and a friend of hers named Ron Goldman. Mr. Simpson was found innocent in 1995 by the jury at his criminal trial. However, a year later he was back in court. The families of his ex-wife and Ron Goldman brought a civil suit against O. J. Simpson. At the end of this civil trial, the jury awarded millions of dollars in compensatory and punitive damages to these families.

Most people favor the jury system. However, it also comes under criticism. Some people criticize the way juries are selected. Some believe that juries make decisions based on emotion rather than facts or that jurors may not have the education or background to understand some complex legal issues. One serious problem is that if the required number of jurors cannot agree on a decision, it is called a hung jury, and the law requires a new trial with a new jury.

I don't want to leave you with the impression that every legal case is tried in court with a jury in the United States. In fact, only about 20 percent of legal cases actually reach the courts. What happens is that in civil cases, most often the two sides settle their dispute out of court with the aid of their lawyers. And in criminal cases, very often a person accused of a particular crime will plea bargain. What actually happens in plea bargaining is that the accused pleads guilty to a lesser crime. Why is this allowed to happen? This is allowed to happen because there is a large number of civil and criminal cases. If all of these cases went to trial, the courts would be very crowded. If an accused person agrees to plead guilty, there will, of course, be no trial in court. This saves the state time and money. Also, the accused person who plea-bargains often is allowed to do so only if he or she also cooperates with the prosecutor in bringing other criminals to justice. From the accused person's point of view, the sentence might be less severe than if he or she went to trial and were found guilty.

Though what goes on in court is often routine and not exciting to observe, jury trials often have very dramatic moments. In fact, courtroom drama has been the subject of many films made over the years. If you have the opportunity, I would encourage you to watch one or two to get a better idea of how a jury trial works.

III. POSTLISTENING

A. Accuracy Check

1. Under the U.S. legal system, is an accused person guilty until proven innocent or innocent until proven guilty?

2. On which legal system is the U.S. legal system based?

3. How many people are ordinarily on a jury?

4. In a civil case involving property or contracts, who ordinarily decides who is at fault and how much, if any, must be paid in damages?

5. In which kind of trial is the defendant required to testify, civil or criminal?

6. In which kind of trial must the degree of proof be higher, civil or criminal?

7. What is a judge's main responsibility at a trial?

8. What is the jury's main responsibility?

9. What percentage of all legal cases, both civil and criminal, are settled out of court?

10. Why does the state so often allow accused people to plea-bargain?

APPENDIX B: ANSWER KEYS

Unit One | **The Face of the People**

Chapter 1   **The Population**

I. PRELISTENING

B. Vocabulary and Key Concepts

1. census
2. populous
3. race
4. origin
5. geographical distribution
6. made up of
7. comprises
8. relatively/progressively
9. Metropolitan/densely
10. decreased/death rate
11. birth rate/increasing
12. life expectancy

D. Notetaking Preparation

1. Number Notation

a. 18.5 mill.   f. 4%

b. 80%   g. 1990

c. 1/2   h. 40%

d. 13.4 mill.   i. 3/4

e. 2:10   j. 33.1%

2. Rhetorical Cues

a. 3

b. 1

c. 2

d. 5

e. 4

II. LISTENING

A. First Listening

Major Subtopics

ST1 population by race and origin

ST2 geographical distribution

ST3 age and sex

III. POSTLISTENING

A. Accuracy Check

1. People's Republic of China, India
2. 281 mill.
3. Hispanics (12.5%)
4. Texas
5. the South and the West
6. 20%
7. by more than 5 million
8. about 6 years
9. 2.2 years
10. a decreasing birth rate and an increasing life expectancy

Chapter 2   Immigration: Past and Present

I. PRELISTENING

B. Vocabulary and Key Concepts

1. immigrated
2. Natural disasters/droughts/famines
3. persecution
4. settlers/colonists
5. stages
6. widespread unemployment
7. scarcity
8. expanding/citizens
9. failure

10. decrease

11. limited

12. quotas

13. steadily

14. trend

15. skills/unskilled

D. Notetaking Preparation

1. Dates: Teens and Tens

a. 1850

b. 1915

c. the 1840s

d. from 1890 to 1930

e. between 1750 and 1850

f. 1776

g. 1882

h. 1929

i. 1860

j. from approximately 1830 to 1930

2. Language Conventions: Countries and Nationalities

Country	People
France	French
Germany	Germans
Scotland; Ireland	Scotch-Irish
Great Britain	Britons; the British
Denmark	Danes
Norway	Norwegians
Sweden	Swedes
Greece	Greeks
Italy	Italians
Spain	Spaniards
Portugal	Portuguese
China	Chinese
Philippines	Filipinos
Mexico	Mexicans
India	Indians
Russia	Russians
Poland	Poles

The Scandinavian countries are Sweden, Norway, and Denmark. The Southern European countries are Italy, Greece, Spain, and Portugal. The Eastern European countries are Russia and Poland.

II. LISTENING

A. First Listening

Major Subtopics

ST1 the Great Immigration

ST2 reasons for the Great Immigration and why it ended

ST3 immigration situation in the United States today

III. POSTLISTENING

A. Accuracy Check

1. colonists or settlers

2. Dutch, French, German, Scotch-Irish, Blacks

3. The third, 1890–1930

4. Southern Europe and Eastern Europe

5. The population doubled, there was widespread unemployment, and there was a scarcity of farmland.

6. free land, plentiful jobs, and freedom from religious and political persecution

7. the failure of the potato crop in Ireland

8. laws limiting immigration from certain areas, the Great Depression, and World War II

9. They are largely non-European.

10. Industry doesn't need a large number of unskilled workers.

Chapter 3   Americans at Work

I. PRELISTENING

B. Vocabulary and Key Concepts

1. statistics

2. goods producing/service

3. stricter/illegal

4. per capita

5. benefits/health insurance

6. wages/workweek

7. romanticize

8. study/productive

9. rising/opposite

10. outproduce

11. stressed

12. matched

13. stagnated

14. CEOs/profits

15. unions/favor

D. Notetaking Preparation

2. Rhetorical Cues

a. 2

b. 1

c. 3

d. 4

II. LISTENING

A. First Listening

Major Subtopics

ST1 a historical look at work in America

ST2 how U.S. workers are doing today

III. POSTLISTENING

A. Accuracy Check

1. 38%

2. 3%

3. service industries

4. 19% in 1900; 60% in 1999

5. $4,200 in 1900; $33,700 in 1999

6. health insurance

7. U.S. workers

8. They are less stressed (more vacation weeks)

9. No

10. to CEOs, the stock market, and corporate profits

Unit Two	**The American Character**

Chapter 4   Family in the United States

I. PRELISTENING

B. Vocabulary and Key Concepts

1. disintegrating

2. domestic role

3. nature/drastically

4. sensitive barometer

5. predominant configuration

6. commitment/reverence

7. conformity/gender

8. lack/liberation

9. self-fulfillment

10. cohabiting couples

11. tripled/quadrupled

12. decline/initial

13. balance/individualism

14. flexible/on-site

15. mandate/allowances

D. Notetaking Preparation

2. Rhetorical Cues

    a. 2

    b. 5

    c. 3

    d. 1

    e. 4

II. LISTENING

Major Subtopics

ST1 traditional familism: mid-1940s to mid-1960s

ST2 period of individualism: mid-1960s to mid-1980s

ST3 the new familism: mid-1980s to present

III. POSTLISTENING

A. Accuracy Check

1. No, they aren't.

2. declining birth rates, rising divorce rates, discontent of women with domestic role

3. a married couple with children

4. It's closer to self-reliance.

5. sexual revolution, women's liberation, and the movement against the Vietnam War

6. the idealization of career and the drive for self-expression and self-fulfillment

7. Single-parent families tripled; cohabiting couples quadrupled.

8. in the second period

9. commitment to family, equality of men and women, fulfillment

10. quality day care, parental leave, family allowances

I. PRELISTENING

B. Vocabulary and Key Concepts

1. mandatory
2. survey/Protestant
3. modernized
4. values
5. guaranteed
6. establishes
7. underestimated
8. role/played
9. decline/revival
10. conservative
11. controversial/politicized
12. phenomenon
13. secular/authoritarian

D. Notetaking Preparation

1. Commonly Used Symbols and Abbreviations

1. pop. of China > India > U.S.
2. death rt. ↘ + birth rt. ↗ —> ↗ in pop.
3. pop. in U.S. c. 281 mill.
4. some people imm. to U.S. ∵ nat. disasters, e.g., droughts, famines
5. situation diff today ∴ people from Latin Am. + Asia imm to U.S. > from Europe
6. After WWII, most Am. families still trad., i.e., w/ working father, housewife, & children
7. Today many child. raised w/o father in home

2. Rhetorical Cues

a. 2
b. 4
c. 1

d. 3

e. 5

II. LISTENING

A. First Listening

Major Subtopics

ST1 facts and figures

ST2 United States compared to other modernized nations

ST3 increasing role of religion in U.S. politics particularly in recent years

III. POSTLISTENING

A. Accuracy Check

1. The media, e.g., television and movies, usually ignore this part of American culture.

2. Protestants, 52%, Catholics, 24%

3. Immigrants to America came from many different countries and religious backgrounds.

4. the United States, 60%; Italy, 7%; France, 4%

5. freedom of worship (religion)

6. that church and state must be kept separate

7. conservative

8. the "rise of the religious right"

9. abortion and prayer in public schools

10. more secular

Chapter 6   Passages: Birth Marriage and Death

I. PRELISTENING

B. Vocabulary and Key Concepts

1. bewildering/ingrained

2. shower/expectant

3. mother-to-be/pretext

4. expressions of envy/reassured

5. unheard of

6. banished/delivery

7. baptism

8. observed/fiancées

9. empowered/civil

10. bride/groom/superstitious

11. banned/hazardous

12. cremated

13. memorial/wake

14. eulogy/deceased

15. condolences/bereaved

III. POSTLISTENING

A. Accuracy Check

1. shortly before the baby is due

2. (1) baby showers not always a surprise, and (2) men sometimes attend

3. baptism

4. the bride's family

5. a religious ceremony

6. something old, something new, something borrowed, and something blue

7. the groom

8. in case of cremation

9. a sympathy card and flowers

10. white

Unit Three | **American Trademarks**

Chapter 7   Multiculturalism

I. PRELISTENING

B. Vocabulary and Key Concepts

1. skeptically/homogeneous

2. deny/impact

3. melting/metaphor

4. alloy/myth

5. excluded/discrimination

6. viewed/prejudice

7. mosaic/autonomous

8. Intermarriage/adoption

9. implied/exception

10. inherit/absorb

11. assimilation/generation

12. fragmentation/proponents

13. dominant/reflects

14. Opponents/Latinos

D. Notetaking Preparation

2. Rhetorical Cues

a. however; on the other hand

b. In fact

c. For instance

d. however; nevertheless

e. Rather; Instead

f. On the other hand; However; Nevertheless

g. furthermore; also

II. LISTENING

A. First Listening

Major Subtopics

ST1 the monoculturalist view

ST2 the multiculturalist view

ST3 the pluralistic view

III. POSTLISTENING

A. Accuracy Check

1. No
2. harder
3. the monoculturalist view
4. African, Asian, and Native Americans as well as each newly arrived group
5. the patchwork quilt
6. No
7. 17%
8. We inherit, absorb, and choose it.
9. fragmentation or destruction of U.S. culture
10. open to change

Chapter 8   Crime and Violence in the United States

I. PRELISTENING

B. Vocabulary and Key Concepts

1. violent/aggravated
2. enforcement/stringent
3. white-collar/embezzlement
4. aggressive/predisposed to
5. to blame/shortcomings
6. root/proliferation
7. deprived of/strike out
8. underclass/disproportionately
9. curbs/socializing
10. values/compassion
11. conscience/bring up
12. punishment/deterrent
13. financiers/lacking
14. takes over/leads to
15. benefits/take for granted

D. Notetaking Preparation

1. Structuring

    a. Crime statistics match public's perception of less crime

    b. Three secondary support ideas:
        1. 1994–2001: violent crime decreased 52%
        2. possible reasons for decrease
        3. statistics on white-collar crime (embezzlement, bribery, etc.) not as clear

    c. Two details for each point.
        1. 1994: 51 victims per 1,000/in 2001, 24 victims per 1,000
        2. stricter law enforcement in cities/stringent penalties on repeat offenders
        3. statistics hard to get and/It doesn't scare people

2. Rhetorical Cues

a. 2	**d.** 6
b. 5	**e.** 3
c. 1	**f.** 4

II. LISTENING

A. First Listening

Major Subtopics

ST1 liberal theory of crime

ST2 conservative theory of crime

ST3 some solutions to the crime problem in the U.S.

III. POSTLISTENING

A. Accuracy Check

1. 52%

2. embezzlement, bribery, political corruption, and/or dangerous corporate policies

3. racism, poverty, and injustice

4. No

5. the liberal theory

6. by giving them values, a conscience

7. socialization by the family and fear of punishment

8. They've enjoyed the benefits of society.

9. good education, health care, and employment

10. conservative

Chapter 9   Globalization

I. PRELISTENING

B. Vocabulary and Key Concepts

1. gross national product

2. acceleration/intensification

3. ignites/skeptics

4. advantage/capitalistic

5. flow of goods

6. driving force

7. currency/tariffs

8. Patents/privatize

9. hamper/integrated

10. benefited/oversimplified

11. engage/achieve

12. protectionist/infringements/investment

13. spoke out/subsidies

14. abolish/speak up

D. Notetaking Preparation

1. Structuring

[Notes]

Poor countries get bad advice or must follow unrealistic rules.

♦ Adjust value of currency

♦ Eliminate tariffs

♦ Pressured to respect patents, copyright laws

  -Patents protect Western technology

  -They keep technology from poor countries

♦ Privatize banks, industries

      -Privatization = govt. sells these to private companies

♦ Encouraged not to subsidize own goods

2. Rhetorical Cues

a. 3

b. 4

c. 1

d. 5

e. 2

II. LISTENING

A. First Listening

Major Subtopics

Intro: definition of globalization, concrete examples

ST1 objections to globalization

ST2 countries where globalization has succeeded

ST3 concrete objections and possible solutions

Conclusion: Future of globalization

III. POSTLISTENING

A. Accuracy Check

1. internationally

2. an economic process

3. environmentalists, unionists, anarchists, some governments, and others

4. technology

5. China, India, South Korea, Taiwan

6. in different ways

7. working conditions in sweatshops and child labor

8. yes

9. the result

10. 23

Chapter 10   Public Education: Philosophy and Funding

I. PRELISTENING

B. Vocabulary and Key Concepts

1. compulsory
2. secular
3. curriculum/standardized
4. funds/handicapped
5. exercised locally
6. elected
7. fluctuates
8. a great degree
9. controversial
10. nonsectarian/compete
11. contract/accountable
12. Supporters
13. Opponents/violates
14. bill/"adequate yearly progress"

D. Notetaking Preparation

1. Structuring: Outlining

ST1 Three levels of control
    A. State department of education
        1. Sets basic curriculum
        2. Sets number of credits
    B. School district
        1. Numbers depend on size of population and state
        2. Responsibilities
            a. Specific content of courses
            b. Decides electives
            c. Operation of schools
    C. Individual schools
        1. Teachers' responsibilities
            a. Deciding how to teach
            b. Preparing and giving examinations

2. Rhetorical Cues

    a. 1

    b. 5

    c. 4

    d. 2

    e. 6

    f. 3

II. LISTENING

A. First Listening

Major Subtopics

ST1 three levels of control

ST2 how funding contributes to local control

ST3 three issues related to funding

III. POSTLISTENING

A. Accuracy Check

1. no nationwide curriculum set by the government, no nationwide examination set by the government

2. state department of education, the school districts, individual schools

3. basic curriculum requirements/a number of credits

4. They are elected by the citizens of a school district.

5. federal government—7%; state government—49%; local school district—44%

6. religious organizations

7. nineteenth century

8. charter schools

9. private schools (usually religious schools)

10. as a dangerous step away from local control of schools

I. PRELISTENING

B. Vocabulary and Key Concepts

1. Postsecondary/community/coeducational

2. accredited/standards

3. prestigious/competitive

4. transcript/standardized

5. extracurricular/ethnic background

6. were enrolled

7. break down/proportions

8. upgrade/skills

9. well versed/well informed

10. lenient/transfer

D. Notetaking Preparation

1. Structuring: Listening

ST3 Community colleges differ from four-year colleges.
    A. Admissions requirements are much more lenient.
        1. Enough to graduate from high school
    B. Cheaper to attend
        1. Tuition and fees are lower
        2. Most students live at home
    C. Two-year programs
        1. Lead to A.A. degree
        2. Many programs vocational but not all

Conclusion: Different purposes—some part-time for interest, others full-time prior to transfer

II. LISTENING

A. First Listening

Major Subtopics

1. facts and figures

2. admissions requirements vary greatly

3. community colleges differ from four-year colleges

4. makeup of student body

III. POSTLISTENING

A. Accuracy Check

1. 4,182
2. from less than 100 to more than 50,000
3. from less than $5,000 to as much as 30 or 40 thousand dollars
4. high school transcripts of grades and test results from a standardized exam such as the SAT
5. GRE, GMAT, and/or LSAT
6. extracurriculur activities, ethnic background, and/or work experience
7. yes
8. Associate of Arts
9. 65.2%
10. 42.6%

Chapter 12   Distance Education

I. PRELISTENING

B. Vocabulary and Key Concepts

1. setting foot
2. instruction/separated
3. correspondence
4. accredited/community
5. upgrade/continuous
6. budget crunches
7. access/technology
8. modes/vary
9. via mail/download
10. residency
11. dropout/traditional
12. unscrupulous/alluring
13. credentials

D. Notetaking Preparation

1. Deciphering Notes

a. No, many distance education programs have residency requirements.

b. No, admission requirements are the same as for on-campus programs.

c. Three examples of computer requirements that online study might require are the latest version of Windows, a microphone, and a modem. (Answers may vary.)

d. Students are more likely to complete traditional programs than distance education programs. (Dropout rate is higher for distance education.)

2. Rhetorical Cues

a. 2   **d.** 6

b. 5   **e.** 3

c. 1   **f.** 4

II. LISTENING

A. First Listening

Major Subtopics

ST1 reasons why distance education is growing so rapidly

ST2 how distance education works, that is, what the modes of delivery are

ST3 some things people considering distance education need to be aware of

III. POSTLISTENING

A. Accuracy Check

1. by time and by distance

2. by correspondence (by mail)

3. 1892

4. 90%

5. at the same time

6. (Answers may vary.)

7. No (There are time limits.)

8. No (They are about the same.)

9. cable modem, DSL

10. No (The dropout rate is higher for distance education courses and programs.)

| Unit Five | **The Official Side** |

Chapter 13   The Role of Government in the Economy

I. PRELISTENING

B. Vocabulary and Key Concepts

1. ownership/property

2. free enterprise

3. interfere/laissez-faire

4. contracts/national defense

5. control/comply with

6. income/public assistance/welfare

7. competitive/antitrust/monopoly

8. stability

9. taxation/inflation

10. unemployment/balance

11. expenditures/interest

12. conservative/favor

13. static/composition

D. Notetaking Preparation

1. Prelecture Reading

a. No. They were suspicious of strong central government.

b. The Confederation was unable to solve many problems facing the new nation and needed a stronger central government.

c. None. In a laissez-faire economy, the government does not interfere with the economy.

d. The government imposed an income tax for the first time. After the Civil War, the government had money for internal improvements to the country.

e. The government usually took the side of big business.

　　　f. It provided employment for large numbers of unemployed people and welfare for others, and instituted the Social Security system

2. Rhetorical Cues

　　　a. 4

　　　b. 5

　　　c. 1

　　　d. 7

　　　e. 2

　　　f. 6

　　　g. 3

II. LISTENING

A. First Listening

Major Subtopics

　　　ST1 to protect the environment

　　　ST2 to help people

　　　ST3 to keep the marketplace competitive

　　　ST4 to maintain economic stability

III. POSTLISTENING

A. Accuracy Check

1. songs, poems, books, inventions

2. The freedom to produce, buy, and sell goods and labor without government intervention.

3. laws governing contracts and property rights; national defense; and providing such things as roads and canals

4. greater

5. to protect it

6. They are too young, old, or sick.

7. a good thing

8. the telephone company [AT&T]

9. taxation, expenditure, and controlling the interest rate on money it lends to businesses

10. It raises it.

Chapter 14   Government by Constitution

I. PRELISTENING

B. Vocabulary and Key Concepts (Script)

1. division/checks/balances
2. branches/legislative/judicial
3. enacting/enforced
4. accused of breaking/legal dispute
5. trials/consistent with
6. tasks/abuse
7. power of veto
8. override/put an end to
9. suspected/resigned
10. unconstitutional/legal
11. civil rights/racial discrimination
12. desegregation
13. nominates a candidate/approve
14. balance of power

D. Notetaking Preparation

1. Prelecture Reading

a. Judicial review is the power of the judicial branch of government to examine and determine the constitutionality of laws passed by the legislative branch.

b. No, it is not explicitly mentioned in the Constitution. The Supreme Court interpreted the Constitution to mean that it had this power in a famous case, *Marbury* v. *Madison,* in 1803.

c. Britain

d. They exercise it less frequently. Although both countries have provisions for judicial review, they are reluctant to use it.

II. LISTENING

A. First Listening

Model Organization

I. Three branches of government

II. Principles of the Constitution
   A. Division of powers
   B. Checks and balances
      1. (examples)
      2. (etc.)

III. POSTLISTENING

A. Accuracy Check

1. It's the oldest constitution that has been in continuous use. [It has been in continuous use for over 200 years.]

2. executive, legislative, and judicial

3. to see that laws enacted by Congress are carried out [executed]

4. the president

5. Each branch of the government has a way to check, or control, one of the other branches of government.

6. If the president vetoes a law, he refuses to sign it.

7. He usually has put an end to the law.

8. by investigating what it considers to be possible illegal activities of the executive branch

9. He might have been removed from office.

10. Although the president nominates candidates to the Supreme Court, Congress must approve his selections.

Chapter 15   Common Law and the Jury System

I. PRELISTENING

B. Vocabulary and Key Concepts

1. guilty/unjustly

2. innocent until proven guilty

3. code of laws

4. common law/precedents

5. testimony/verdict

6. private parties

7. compensatory/punitive damages

8. "beyond a reasonable doubt"

9. convicted

10. irrelevant/evidence/admissible

11. hung

12. pleads guilty/lesser crime

D. Notetaking Preparation

1. Prelecture Reading

a. no

b. Mary Beth Whitehead-Gould

c. 2

d. no

e. Because of the nature of the law, courts will be obligated to base future decisions on decisions made in this case.

2. Courtroom Language

a. court reporter

b. judge

c. witness

d. jury

e. bailiff

f. defendant

g. plaintiff/prosecutor

h. courtroom clerk

III. POSTLISTENING

A. Accuracy Check

1. innocent until proven guilty

2. British common law

3. 6–12

4. a jury

5. civil

6. criminal

7. to see that the trial is conducted according to law

8. to decide whether they believe the testimony they hear and whether the evidence presented to them is valid

9. about 80%

10. because it's difficult to prove people are guilty and because trials are so expensive to conduct

PHOTO CREDITS

Chapter 12

Page 121 top: © Frank Siteman/PhotoEdit—All rights reserved;   **Page 121 bottom:** © Spencer Grant/PhotoEdit—All rights reserved.

UNIT 5 OPENER

Page 133: © Ron Ruhoff/Index Stock Imagery.

Chapter 13

Page 134: 13.1: © Joseph Sohm; Visions of America/CORBIS.

Chapter 14

Page 145 top: © Grantpix/Index Stock Imagery;   **Page 145 center:** © Royalty-Free/CORBIS; **Page 145 bottom:** © Jacob Halaska/Index Stock Imagery;   **Page 150 left:** © Brand X/Getty Images; **Page 150 center:** © DAVID SCULL/Bloomberg News/Landov;   **Page 150 right:** © Jason Reed/Reuters Newmedia Inc./CORBIS.

Chapter 15

Page 155: © John Neubauer/PhotoEdit—All rights reserved.